THE VAPE SHOP MANUAL

The Comprehensive guide to starting a successful Vape Shop

By Sham Shivaie

Shamim Shivaie
Sham@VapeAboutit.Com

Ordering Information:
Quantity sales. Special discounts are available on quantity purchases by corporations, associations, and others. For details, contact the publisher at the address above.
Orders by U.S. trade bookstores and wholesalers.

First printing, 2016

ISBN-13: 978-1530334445
ISBN-10: 1530334446

Table of Contents

Introduction 1

  How to use this book.. 2

  My background 5

  My journey as a Vaper.. 7

  Why I wrote this book.. 9

Module 1: Planning Your Vape Shop................ 13

  Chapter 1: What it Takes to Open a Shop............ 15

    So you want to open a vape shop?........................... 15

    The truth of the matter is… 17

    First things first 22

  Chapter 2: Visualizing Success 27

    You need a vision.. 27

    The plan 28

    Research.. 31

    Business Structure 33

  Chapter 3: Create Your Brand...............................37

    Your name Your Image.. 37

    Marketing Strategy:... 40

    SWOT analysis 43

Module 2 49

  Chapter 4: Realizing Your Vision 51

    Opening your vape shop 52

    Politics 54

    Finding the right location... 56

    Signing the lease.. 64

  Chapter 5: Final Preparation 69

    Budgeting your store.. 69

    Services 72

    Lay Out 76

    Product Over view 82

Chapter 6: The Global Phenomena 85
   Industry Overview 85
   Tip of the iceberg 87
   Vendor/Distributor Overview 88
   E-liquid 93
   Concerning vaporizers and cannabis 97

Chapter 7: Stocking Up 103
   How to purchase your starting inventory 103
   Keep it simple 108
   Selecting flavors 110

Module 3: Operating Your Store 115
Chapter 8: Running Your Shop 117
   Management 118
   Dealing with Partners 122
   Customer Service 123

Chapter 9: Sales Strategies for Success 133
   Selling to customers 133
   The structure of selling 136
   Sampling Liquid 140
   Referrals 142

Chapter 10: Marketing 147
   Marketing your vape shop 147
   Social Media/online marketing 149
   Advertising 150
   Building awareness 152
   The secret to getting followers 155
   ABM: Always be Marketing 157

Chapter 11: Wishing You the Best 159
   Advocacy - last but definitely not the least 159
   Wishing you the best 161

Welcome,

First and foremost, I would like to thank you for your purchase. More importantly I would like to congratulate you for taking the first step towards accomplishing your goal of opening a vapor shop. By making the decision to invest your time, and money into this book. You are taking the first step towards success.

I think anybody who is an avid vaper has had the idea and desire to get into this industry. But there is a big difference between taking action and daydreaming. So I commend you for actually taking action.

It is my sincerest hope this book will serve as a blueprint towards realizing your vision of becoming a vape shop owner. This book contains the tips, steps and knowledge needed to open your first store. Along with some useful do's and don'ts I have learned from my own experiences.

You are about to start on a journey, that I hope will lead from where you are now, to becoming a successful and prosperous "**Vaporpreneur**".

<u>The purpose of this book is to transform your ambitions, ideas and vision into a thriving vape shop.</u> This book will cover everything you need to know, to take you from point A to Z, it contains the knowledge you need to guide you from the idea phase that you are currently in right now, to opening day of your store.

We are at the beginning of a revolution that has so many widespread implications and endless opportunities. It almost hurts my head sometimes to think just what an impact vaping can have on the world. It has the potential to impact the economy, improve the environment and save countless lives. In my opinion not since the internet, has there been a technology that can have such a widespread impact.

By making the decision to get into this industry, you are not only seizing an opportunity to achieve massive financial success. But you're also helping contribute to the rise and dominance of this industry as a whole. Best of all you couldn't have picked a better time. Sure it may seem like vape shops are everywhere nowadays. But when you look at the numbers, the truth is we are barely scratching the surface.

But before we get out the champagne and celebrate, there is still a long road ahead of us. Yes there is a gold mine that awaits, but that gold must still be mined.

There is a lot, I repeat **A LOT** of work ahead for those of us getting into the industry at this pointin time. The payoff is limitless, but there are many challenges and obstacles to overcome along the way.

This is a true ground floor opportunity, and it will remain so, even for the next few years to come. With only government regulation the only real threat to stopping its momentum. Your decision to get involved now, is positioning yourself to ride the giant tidal wave of growth that we are at the precedent of. By taking action today, you are positioning yourself to succeed, and thrive as the vapor industry matures and expands.

How to use this book:

The purpose of this book is simple:

To serve as a comprehensive guide on how to open a vape shop.

It is a guide that covers all the ins and outs of the steps necessary to open your a store. It covers crucial topics that will make a big difference in your level of success. While also helping educate you on key subjects that any business owner should know. The format of this book was designed to provide an effective balance of theory along with   technical step-by-step direction. I have strived to answer all the questions a first time store owner may have. While also providing insights from my own experiences and observation.

The structure of this book is linear, but also set up in a way that has key topics self-contained. Allowing you to come back to it, and use it as a reference. But I strongly suggest you don't just glance over or skim through sections you feel like you may already know or have experience in.

For example: The section on product knowledge; even if you are an expert builder with a solid understanding of how everything works, I still advise you read through it. Because it's written in a way that you can use to easily explain to customers that are beginners.

Also if you have sales experience or a marketing background, I still suggest you go over the material in that section. We not only break down important marketing principles but how they apply specifically to a vapor shop.

Positioned throughout the book are useful exercises designed to help you better understand the material, and apply it in a way that's tailored to your individual needs.

This book is comprised of 3 modules, with corresponding sections within each one.

Modules:

1. Planning to open your store
2. Opening your store
3. Operating your store

In module 1 we cover things like creating your business plan, and scouting for locations. Module 2 focuses in detail on how to set up your inventory, and make your first large purchase of merchandise. We finish out the remainder of the book in Module 3 focusing on how to operate and market your shop once it opens.

How to get the most out of this book:

I suggest you and your founding team read this book in its entirety once, and take note of key areas of interest. Then while you're applying the material in the process of opening your shop, read through once again.

I've found that to truly absorb the information in a book it requires more than one read. Also please don't skip out on the exercises, they're designed to help you focus and define your goals. In my experience one of the most powerful keys to success is clarity. Clearly defined goals and ideas can make all the difference. Clarity in what you want helps you stay focused and on track towards accomplishing your goals.

Sure, we all want to be successful, but how do you define success for yourself? The exercises provided will help you gain that clarity.

So who am I, and why the heck should you listen to me?

Like yourself, I am someone that had the bright idea one day to open a vape shop. Like yourself, I saw the opportunity and the wheels started turning and I'm proud to say, I've turned that idea into a reality. Being in this industry has truly been a life altering and amazing journey.

But along with my successes, I've also experienced massive set backs, including having two stores shut down by city government. Which is even more reason to listen to me, because I've definitely had some downs to go with my ups. **My intention with this book, isn't just to teach you what to do, but also what NOT to do.**

I still currently own and operate a brick and mortar retail shop, and although I'm placing more time these days on expanding my companies as a whole. I still make sure to allocate time daily for working on the sales floor of my shop, and interacting with customers.

This is especially important when it comes to my work as a consultant, because it allows me to get a first person view on the needs and requirements to successfully operate a retail shop. **I know what it's like to be in the trenches of vapor shop retail**, because I'm in them every day, 7 days a week.

Since opening my first shop, I have expanded into other areas in the industry. I started the digital media company Vape About It (www.vapeaboutit.com) and am proud to say it has quickly become the go to source for news in the vape industry, now with a global readership. I have my own e-liquid company (www. VapeologyCo.com), and most recently started Vaporpreneur (www.Vaporpreneur.com) which is a full service consulting group for the vape industry.

I'm also very proud to be be involved in vape advocacy and having the opportunity to help the brave hard working advocates that are fighting daily on the industry's behalf.

My background:

One of my pet peeves when reading business books is when the author continuously talks about themselves, so with that said I'll try to keep it at a minimum except for sharing personal experiences. But I believe credibility is important as well:

I've always wanted to be an entrepreneur, it's in my blood. Both my parents have started and successfully ran their own companies. I started my first business when I was 16, and haven't stopped since.

I got into night life promotion when i was 19, which is funny considering you have to be 21 to get into clubs. That business evolved into a full event planning company. At 21 I invested money I had saved up into buying my martial arts studio from its former owner.

By 22 I suffered my first major failure, as that martial arts school failed and I found myself dead broke. But out of that failure came a major turning point for me in my career, which lead me into consulting.

I was frustrated and upset about my failure so I threw myself into learning everything and anything I could about "business". I devoured book after book, went to seminars, listened to audio books etc. I literally got obsessed with acquiring as much knowledge about business,marketing, sales and entrepreneurship as I could. So that the next time I started a business, I would succeed, and succeed big.

Birds of a feather flock together as they say, and most my friends were young entrepreneurs and business owners as well. I found myself spending hours giving them advice, helping them with marketing, etc. One day my friend handed me a check for $500, thanking me for helping him re-do his marketing strategy. He told me my input had doubled his profits in the last month alone. I thought to myself, "wait a minute! I can get paid for this ?".

As I grew in reputation, it only amplified my thirst for knowledge; I had the cash flow to invest even more into my self-education. I was working on my business degree during the week, but on weekends I was always at a seminar or workshop learning whatever I could. Everything from sales, leadership, online marketing, direct marketing, and copywriting, you name it. I spent hours learning and researching. Eventually settled on marketing as my main focus, which soon evolved into product development for start ups. I found what I enjoyed the most was helping a business start, and helping it create a brand.

But soon I found my entrepreneurial drive itching, yes I loved consulting on other people's businesses, but I was really craving to start my own business. Even though my consulting company was a business in itself, I used to joke that my "business was business" but I missed the thrill of starting my own company from scratch.

I was also burnt out from the tech/start up industry in San Francisco, so I wanted to do something different, more people oriented.

In the summer of 2012, I started a hookah catering company,which I thought it was a more innovative idea to offer a "mobile hookah bar" for events, than opening a lounge.

then In the winter of 2012 an acquaintance who was referred by a mutual friend contacted me about consulting for him as he started a food truck .

I found the opportunity interesting because the food truck industry was exploding with growth, and was emerging as the fastest growing sector in the restaurant industry.

The project quickly turned into a partnership, and I came on board to handle marketing and business operations, while my partner handled the day to day/kitchen. We found quick success and by summer of 2013 we also started our own food truck park and catering service.

I loved the food truck industry, but food business wasn't really my thing, I wanted something I was truly passionate about. Throughout this time, since I was 18 I had maintained a strong pack a day smoking habit.

Sure I tried to quit, but I never really stuck with it. By the age of 27 I had a pack and a half daily smoking habit. Not to mention I had also opened a full scale hookah lounge. So I was literally inhaling smoke around the clock, which certainly didn't take long to make a negative impact on my health.

My journey as a Vaper.

I woke up one sunny summer morning and couldn't breathe. No literally I was not able to get enough oxygen, I felt like I was suffocating. I quickly went to the hospital, and after running tests my doctor informed me I had early symptoms of COPD. Which isn't even normal at such a young age. Needless to say, I quit smoking on the spot, I didn't even have a last cigarette. But the craving for nicotine and going cold turkey had me stressed out constantly.

I knew about e-cigs, I had even tried a few of those awful cigalikes. My friend and fellow smoking buddy had purchased an Ego 650 starter kit and he seemed to be having good luck with it. So I figured I'd give it a try because vaping didn't seem to harm my breathing or hurt my lungs.

I went online to buy a "vape" but was so confused by all the options. I spent that night reading up online, researching on what to get but was still frustrated. I called my friend and he suggested we go to the vapor shop he had gone to.

I'll never forget the first time I stepped into that store, the unique "vape shop smell" the culmination of 100 different flavor scents combined into its own delicious aroma, unique to only vape shops.

I remember my excitement to try all the different flavors and my curiosity about the different batteries and tanks. But in the end, not only did I end up wasting money, I ended up having to go back 3 times to that store in just the first week because the staff there never spent the time to teach me how to properly use my set up. Even my friend said, "yeah I just went online and taught myself".

I was so frustrated with the experience, I tried another nearby store and the same thing, poor customer service, lack of attentiveness, and very overpriced. Ironically, although I was frustrated with the shopping experience, I was quickly getting obsessed with vaping. Just like I did before with learning about business, I spent hours reading up on it. Not just on how to vape, but the industry itself, the opportunity and the potential impact it could have on people's health. I also found my breathing started to improve, and I was no longer craving cigarettes.

As a business consultant, you reach a point where every time you're in a business you naturally analyze, and evaluate it. I thought about the terrible experience at the stores I went to, I thought, I can't be the only one, how many other people must have had this problems? I also thought about how I probably would have just given up and gone back to smoking had it not been for the health risk.

How many people have given up on vaping because these stores don't apply better business practices? Although I didn't know everything I needed to know about vaping, I did have the experience and knowledge on how to start and run a business. So I decided then and there that I would open my own store.

Why I wrote this book:

I've always loved consulting, I love coming up with new ideas, evaluating problems and finding solutions. Then taking those ideas and applying them to business. I enjoy the strategy and problem solving not to mention the creativity.

More so I love the ability to work in various different kinds of business at once. I think it's solving the puzzle that I enjoy the most, along with taking an idea and making it tangible. I'm truly passionate about entrepreneurship and business, it's not really work to me, more like a creative passion.

My other passion of course is the vapor industry. I don't view vaping as just a business, but a mission. I believe we have an opportunity here to make a very powerful, positive impact on the world, and I'm truly devoted to that mission.

As an entrepreneur, I love the opportunity to be able to help pioneer a worldwide industry, thats a very rare opportunity in business.

I also love the community as a whole, I love the hobbyist component, and what's better than the feeling you get when you discover a new flavor that tastes amazing?

But everything aside... **it's the mission: the potential for saving lives that I find the most inspiring.**

This book was written to fill a need, the need for a comprehensive blueprint to help aspiring **vaporpreneurs** who want to join in that mission and take up this cause. In every industry there are numerous books and guides on how to get started. If you want to open a restaurant there is a book for that, build your own app? there is a book for that.

I felt the Vapor industry needs one too, so I wrote this not only to try and help aspiring store owners as they're getting started. But to also help guide their transition from vape enthusiast to vapor entrepreneur.

I hope this book will fill that need and serve as the blueprint for future store owners. I'm very excited for what the future holds in our industry, and feel truly blessed to have the opportunity to contribute to it. I hope you enjoy my work, and would love to hear your feedback.

Feel free to share your thoughts, feed back and any ideas, contact me directly at: Sham@vaporpreneur.com

Knowledge is power:

This book will provide you with the information and tools you need to successfully open a vape shop. But by no means does that mean you should stop learning about business. One of the biggest differences between successful entrepreneurs is their commitment to learning; they put time and energy into reading, and increasing their knowledge.

I strongly encourage you to commit yourself to continuously learning and improving yourself as an entrepreneur. Read books, read blogs, commit to learning. Not only will it improve your performance and success as a vaporpreneur but it will also help you grow and improve as a person overall.

There are countless books on business theory, marketing, sales, leadership etc. Reading about these topics adds more tools to your toolbox. Tools that you can use to grow your business. Also do your best to encourage your partners, and employees to learn as well. You want your team to perform at their best. Pushing them to devote time to learning is the most effective way of ensuring you will have a team of superstars.

Pro Tip:

Personally, as a general policy I challenge all my team members to read a book that I assign every month. We read it together, and have a meeting every month to discuss what we've learned. It's a powerful team building exercise that pushes us all to learn and improve ourselves.

There is an old saying that "leaders are readers", and although the quote sounds novel, it couldn't be closer to the truth.

If you look at all the great entrepreneurs of the past, they all devoted time to improve themselves and learn. As a store owner you are stepping into the role of a leader. Not only a leader for your staff, but a leader for the industry.

So without further ado and ranting by me, let's get started shall we? ...

Module 1:
Planning Your Vape Shop

Chapter 1:
What it Takes to Open a Shop

So you want to open a vape shop?

Congratulations, you're about to join one of the fastest growing industries. Vaping has exploded with growth in just the last few years, and best of all this is just the tip of the iceberg.

Specialty vapor retail stores are a huge opportunity. Demand for an in person shopping experience has never been higher.

A vape shop isn't just a retail store, it's an interaction point for vapers to engage with the vape community. This is a big theme I'm going to keep repeating over the course of the book. Because that gives brick and mortar a big advantage over online retailers

But first Answer this question...

What's the reason you want to open a vape shop?

Is it because of a genuine passion for vaping? Is it because you love the community, and you find it a motivating mission to help make vapor products accessible to your community? Is it because you truly believe vaping can make a huge impact on people's quality of life and health by providing a solution to quit smoking? Or is it because you think it can make money?

<u>Is your motivation for getting into this industry out of passion or just because see the big dollar opportunities?</u>

Now to clarify, I am not suggesting the profit potential shouldn't be a factor. At the end of the day, if you're opening a business, the goal is to make money. But the point I'm trying to make is that making money should not be your **only** reason. There is a very big difference between opening a business you truly love, with the hope of achieving financial success and opening a business you think is just great income opportunity.

You have to be genuinely passionate about this industry and community. A vape store is not just a brick and mortar retail space that people go to buy vapes or e-liquid. It is literally a hub for the community, it's the focal point "vapers" go to interact and socialize. It's more than just a place to buy stuff, because they can buy the same items online, it's the experience they're after.

The reason vape shops are so lucrative and growing is because unlike a clothing boutique for example, a vape shop serves far more of a purpose than a simple retail destination.

<u>A successful vape shop is a combination of retail store, social club, repair shop and classroom.</u>

People come to get education and learn about vaping. Whether it's a beginner looking to switch from cigarettes, or a hardcore dripper who wants a unique build for their atty. They come to try new liquids, to see new products. **All in all; a successful vape shop has to provide more than just "stuff to buy", it has to provide an experience, and that experience has to be good enough to get them coming back.**

So you have to answer the question, what is your real intention for wanting to get into this industry? If you just want to make money, I suggest looking at the millions of other money making opportunities out there. Opening a vape shop isn't difficult, but opening a **<u>successful</u>** vape shop is. Success in this industry requires a love for all that vaping represents, and a strong desire to help make a positive impact on people's lives.

Far too often I've had people approach me telling me how *"they want to open a vape shop"* and asking for my advice. This is always the very first question I ask. Because it's the most important question, it's the question that truly matters.

You don't have to know everything there is to know about vaping, I opened my first shop barely knowing everything I should have regarding products. Nor do you have to be a retail expert, or a marketing guru. Sure those things help, but those are all skills you can learn, or find talented people to help you with.

No, you don't need to be a serial entrepreneur with years of experience. Those won't determine your success more than your intention will. **The most important thing you need; is a true passion for vaping**. The biggest factor that will determine your success aside from your work ethic is your intention for having a vape shop.

So what is the answer? What is the reason you want to get into this industry? Give it some thought, you don't have to answer right away. At the end of this section you're going to have to write your answer. It doesn't have to be long, but you need to have a clearly defined intention, a personal mission statement if you will.

The truth of the matter is...

The reason why I place so much importance on having genuine passion for the industry and community is for one very overlooked reason...

This is not an easy business.

Oh sure it may look like a lot of fun, and trust me it is lots of fun. But that fun also comes with a lot of hard work, and the business model itself isn't easy.

One of the biggest misconceptions is the amount of work and organization required to run a vapor shop. Is it the most complicated business in the world? Of course it isn't, not by a long shot. There are far more difficult retail businesses you could do.

But if you think all it takes is a good knowledge of your products and you can just sit back and vape all day while the dollars roll in you are sadly mistaken.

It goes without saying any business requires hard work. It comes with the territory. Especially more so when it comes to brick and mortar retail.

Now I doubt anyone thinks opening a business is a breeze or a relaxing experience. But with vaping it's even more so.

The reason being…

The nature of the vapor industry itself:

Take a clothing store for example, their merchandise and inventory cycles through seasonally. But the vapor industry is in a state of constant expansion, and its only getting bigger, literally by the day. The industry has exploded with growth especially over the last two years. Just as there are new vape shops popping up in cities across the country and around the world. There are new products being developed and released daily, existing products being upgraded, new e-liquid flavors being concocted.

I recall how just in the first year of opening my first store the amount of products exponentially increased. There is no doubt the industry is heavily saturated on numerous levels. From way too many choices in atomizers to far too many e-liquid companies trying to get their piece of shelf space. The industry is booming and with that comes unique pros and cons.

We'll get into inventory and how to determine your merchandise later on in the book. But the reason why you should remember this is because as a store owner and operator; it is your responsibility to keep on top of it.

Now that seems like an overwhelming thought at first, when you realize just how many endless choices there are. But don't worry you will learn an effective system to monitor and stay up to date on everything.

Also I'm not suggesting you have to know and pay attention to every single product out there, because truthfully a huge majority of stuff is redundant, or just copies of each other, and don't even get me started on the clone debate! (don't worry we'll get into it later).

The point is, your role as store owner, is to be gatekeeper of all things vape related. Stay be up to date and constantly be on the look out for the next big product. That's one of the key differences with the vapor business; your inventory is literally in a constant state of influx.

This connects back to what we discussed regarding passion. If you don't truly love the industry, if you don't truly love vaping, then you won't be very motivated to constantly educate yourself on the products will you?

If you look at a Mod and just see a metal tube you can sell for money you won't be very effective as a store operator. But if you look at a Mod as a beautiful piece of art, an instrument that allows you to enjoy an experience you really love, and helps improve your health, then you have the right mindset.

So have I scared you off yet? I hope not, because **the truth is the vapor industry is so fulfilling** on a personal level not to mention financially. Not only can it provide you with financial security, it also allows you to be a part of a passionate community where you'll meet wonderful like-minded people and make great friends.

the community is all about unity, even stores you would think view each other as competition work together to throw events. I've had the opportunity to be a part of a few industries, vaping has a camaraderie I haven't seen elsewhere. But as enjoyable as it is, and as huge of an opportunity it is, you have to go into things knowing the full picture not just what you assume based on what you've seen at your local vape shop.

The biggest mistake I've noticed people make when they get the light bulb moment to open a shop is *"oh I can do it to, how hard can it be"*. Now I admit this isn't exactly brain surgery (although some of the builds out there nowadays might as well be).

But it still does require an understanding of business, an understanding of everything from sales, marketing, customer service, management and supply chain. <u>If you think this is as easy as buying some vapes and e-liquid you are sadly mistaken.</u>

I recall an acquaintance stopping by one of my stores and asked if I could grab lunch because he wanted to talk to me about something. Now I'm pretty accustomed to getting asked to have coffee meetings or lunch, because anytime friends or friends of friends want to start a business they contact me. So I obliged, to be polite and because hey at the very least it was free lunch.

We sat down and placed our orders, and I asked what he wanted to discuss. He began telling me he wanted to open a vapor shop. He had some money saved up and his other friend did too and they wanted to partner together.

He was quick to add he wasn't going to open it anywhere in the areas of my stores and to not worry about competition.

He went on about how he was hoping I'd consult him and provide guidance on what to do. I told him of course I'd help, it sounded like a great idea, and that if done correctly he could definitely succeed.

I told him I was a little surprised because I had no idea he vaped, I mean he had never come into my store before, and he lived local so it threw me off a bit. I was excited to talk shop with him, "A new vapor buddy" I thought. So I asked him what his current setup was. He looked at me blankly and asked "what do you mean?"

I clarified "what's your setup, what are you using to vape right now?" He laughed and said, "oh I don't vape, I don't care to vape myself, I just want open a store because I know you must be making a killing ".

Lets just say I lost my appetite when I heard his answer. But after a long, blunt and honest conversation with him about his prospects of succeeding in the business when he himself doesn't have any interest in it, he realized maybe it wasn't for him.

Which I felt was the right thing to do because even though his answer was a little offending, as an entrepreneur, you never want to see someone risk their money knowing chances are they won't succeed.

Now that's an extreme example, but that wasn't the only time I've heard something similar. The point is; A LOT of people right now want to open a vape shop. But for every genuinely motivated vaper who truly loves this industry and is ready to put in the hard work. There's someone that just see's dollar signs and a money making opportunity.

So again what is your real intention? You want to make money? Fantastic! Go get into stocks or real estate or something else.

Do you actually want to help build an industry that has years and years of growth ahead of it, while making an impact on people's quality of life?

Then lets move forward...

As I mentioned at the start of this section, you're going to write the answer as to why you want to open vapor shop.

Why do you want to get involved in this industry? Can you honestly say that you'll wake up every day happy and excited to open the door to your shop?

Write your answer here and read it out loud, have your business partners do the same. The point of this is to give real clarity as to why you want to do this.

Exercise 1: Get clarity

My Vaporpreneur statement of intent:

I want to open my own vapor shop because ...

First things first

Before we jump into more industry specific information, we definitely need to discuss <u>entrepreneurship</u> as a whole and what it means to own a business.

There's an old saying that truly hits the nail on the head and it goes as follows...

"An entrepreneur is willing to work 80 hours a week in order to avoid working 40 hours a week"

If I was to summarize what it means to be an entrepreneur and to own a business in one sentence that quote is what I would use every time. Because no matter what way you look at, it is the damn honest truth.

<u>Everyone wants to be an entrepreneur:</u>

In my observation as a consultant, and entrepreneur everyone has entertained the thought of owning their own business at some point. Regardless of what walk of life, background or profession they're from, everyone has had an idea for a business. Whether that's opening a gourmet deli selling home made recipes passed down through the years, or building the next big Silicon Valley startup. Everyone has had a light bulb go off in their mind about a business idea they think could be successful.

Now with that said, only a fraction of those people actually pursue it, and an even smaller fraction of people actually follow through completely and transform their idea or concept into a real tangible business.

Entrepreneurship is the only profession that anyone thinks they can do, which also doesn't require any real requirement. That's the beauty of being an entrepreneur, everyone can have a shot at it. You can't just decide "hey I want to be a lawyer" and start practicing law. But anyone can take the risk of starting a business, for better or for worse.

I've also observed with vaping in particular, those who turn it into a full blown hobby start brainstorming on ways to turn it into a business. It's only natural that if you find something you truly enjoy and see others making money with it, you start thinking about how you can do it to.

Vaping takes a hold of some people, it's a very intriguing process to watch. As people get more and more absorbed. Now of course not everyone is like that, in fact the majority of people as you will come to find when you open a store; simply view vaping as a solution to their smoking addiction.

They just want an easy to use product, and good tasting e-liquid. But the ever-growing vaper community is proof of just how infatuated people can become with the culture.

<u>Entrepreneurship is truly a labor of love, because trust me when I tell you, if you don't love your business, you won't put in the required effort necessary to make it succeed</u>. Remember 80 hours a week to avoid working 40 hours a week. We are truly living in the age of entrepreneurship, not that the concept is anything new, not at all. But in the last decade alone we've seen an explosion of motivated individuals building massively successful companies.

Especially with the many advances in technology. Along with the rise of mobile applications, and social networks. Entrepreneurship has become the desired path for most, young and old. Its mainstream now in many ways, you see shows like Shark Tank further spotlighting the entrepreneurial dream and the many success stories of people turning an idea into millions and even billions of dollars.

We are in the age of entrepreneurship, and why shouldn't it be everyone's aspiration? <u>Who doesn't want to be master of their own destiny</u>, to have the freedom to have a career and work life on their own terms.

Who doesn't want to have the feeling of satisfaction and fulfillment that comes with building a successful business? Not to mention the huge stress relief of gaining financial security for yourself and your family.

But as romanticized and cool owning a business sounds, for every success story there are 100 failures. Often times the only difference between the ones who succeeded and failed is the perseverance and hard work put in.

The difference is those who succeeded faced the same obstacles but they didn't give up, and that's the cornerstones of entrepreneurship. That unshakeable perseverance, and not giving up, even when things are bad.

It's pretty easy to be motivated and work hard when you're getting positive results, when the money's rolling in. But can you maintain that level and even step it up a notch when things aren't so good? When things are slow or aren't going the way you want?

The vapor industry is booming, the long term potential that this industry offers are nothing short of mind blowing. There are already a number of people who have started and built successful businesses so far, and we're just getting started. Our industry is still just in the infancy of what it can be. But just because it's a gold rush, doesn't mean everyone who mines is going to strike gold.

Regardless of how good an opportunity sounds there's never a sure thing when it comes to business. I tell you this because it's important you approach this with the mindset that there is no guarantee you'll succeed. There's a very good chance you will, especially if you apply the principles outlined in this book. But as the saying goes, never count your eggs before they hatch.

It is not easy, so before you start the process of planning your soon to be successful vapor store you have to prepare yourself for what it's going to entail.

You will have to work harder than you ever have, and there is no clocking out. That is the one key point I always try and emphasize to anyone starting a business. There is no getting off work.

You are always at work, it is a 24/7 commitment. That doesn't mean you have to be working 24/7, it just means you won't succeed working standard hours.

Entrepreneurs don't have the luxury of clocking in, working their shift, and clocking out. As intense as it sounds, there is no clocking out. Now the upside to that is: you do get to control your schedule, and determine your own career path, but that is the price you pay in exchange for it.

Aside from the financial risk you're taking, you have to also keep one thing in mind, that can definitely help motivate you but you can't disregard. You're not getting a paycheck, you are not getting paid for your hours. This isn't a job, it's a lifestyle, more so in the vapor industry which is literally a lifestyle at this point.

From one end, there's no limit to how much money you can make, but counter to that, you can also work for months without drawing any salary. It all comes down to your results, and your results is going to be greatly determined by your work ethic and consistency with said work ethic.

Owning a business is amazing, it's the greatest career in the world. But it's also frightening, frustrating, upsetting, annoying, and stressful. Again **this is not to discourage you**, I just can't stand business books that only talk about how much money you'll be making, and how it's a cakewalk if you just follow what's in the book.

Being a **vaporpreneur** is a great opportunity; it can be a life changing decision for you, as it has been for me. But it's not all fun and blowing clouds, so with that said if you're ready to work hard, and then work harder. Roll up your sleeves; grab your favorite set up and e-liquid of choice and lets make it happen.

Chapter 2:
Visualizing Success

You need a vision:

Plan your work, and work your plan is a saying that's always worked for me. Success in business is heavily reliant on strategy; in fact I feel strategy is one of the most overlooked things by starting entrepreneurs.

Strategy is smart planning, and execution of that plan. But before we begin the first step of opening your vapor shop and developing your business plan. You need a vision, a vision is the older sibling of a goal, a vision is the big picture, something you want to achieve long term. A vision is a summarizing mission statement that describes what you dream of achieving.

Every successful business starts as an idea, but it's the vision that guides you. Look at it this way: your vision is a desired destination, your plan and strategy is the map on how to get there.

So before we create a map, we need a desired destination. **What is your vision for your vape shop?** What do you want it to be? What do you see when you picture your store 6 months from now? One year from now? 5 years from now? What is your vision for this business?

You don't need to write a novel, but try and make it more detailed than "I want a successful vape shop" course you want a successful vape shop, but how do you define that success?

Create a vision statement that outlines and describes what you wish to achieve with your Vapor Store. Feel free to use mine as an example, but try and customize it for yourself and your own goals.

Vaporpreneur Vision statement:

My vision for my vape shop is to open the most popular store in my city. My store will carry high quality vaping equipment with a wide selection of choices to match my customer's budgets. I will offer at least 60 different flavors and have a stylish tasting bar for customers to sample at. My vision is to create a fun, easy to access shop for everyone in my community that vapes to come and enjoy in a upbeat friendly atmosphere.

I will have comfortable couches for customers to hang out. I will place a big emphasis on providing great customer service. I wish to gross $40,000 a month in sales. This amount will allow me to not only pay my staff a great wage, but will also provide enough income for me to save and achieve financial security.

Exercise 2:

We defined your intention, now its time to create a vision for your business.

Your vision statement:

"My vision for my store is..."

The plan:

What is a business plan?

It is your roadmap to success, and not something you should cut corners on...

The concept of a business plan has changed a lot over the years. It used to be a standard 30 + page document that had to be filled with overly complicated graphs and figures. Then you presented it to potential investors or the bank for a loan.

While business plans are still crucial they don't have to as complicated as they seem. The purpose of a business plan is to provide clarity to your business idea.

Your business plan should answer the following 6 questions:

1. Your core business operation
2. An overview of the industry you're in
3. How your business will be structured
4. What are you going to do to get customers?
5. How much it'll cost to start/operate
6. How much you project it to make

Now don't worry, nothing has to be set in stone, plans always change so don't stress yourself if things aren't exact. Sure you can have all kinds of pretty graphs, and figures, cite an endless array of useful facts. But none of that matters if you don't answer those core 6 questions.

The question I get asked a lot is, what if I'm paying for things myself. If I'm self-funding, with no loan and investors do I still need a business plan?

The answer is:

If you're putting your own money in and taking all the risk yourself, then it's **even more important for you to create a detailed business plan**.

Even if no other eyes but your own will see it, it's still imperative. You can't hit a target you can't see, and a business plan defines your target. Maybe you have a very clear idea of what you want your shop to be, but you still need that map to help guide your way. It's the most efficient way to organize your overall vision and concept. More so, it can also serve as a tool to evaluate your progress and make sure you're staying on track. **Not only is it your road map, but it also serves as your compass**.

So we've established the key 6 points your business plan must touch on. So now lets go over some of the core fundamentals of a business plan:

Afterwards you will review a basic template you can use to begin writing your own. A plan for a plan if you will.

Note: I haven't included a sample business plan in this book. Because aside from it being totally cliché, It's also kind of useless. Most "example" business plans are over stuffed with needless information that are just there to fill up pages in a book. The business plan template is really all you need to create a solid and effective plan.

If you really feel that you need to see examples, there's plenty online to see, but don't fall into the trap of trying to make yours longer than necessary.

You might think an investor may want to see as much information as possible, but in truth they don't. <u>In my experience it can actually work against you if your presentation is too long, and redundant.</u>

In fact it might piss them off that you expect them to read through so much. I remember sitting in on a pitch once. A client of mine did angel investing, in walks in a guy and his business partner for the pitch. They handed us this massive, thick binder full of pages that was their business plan. My client took one look, and told them he's not interested in investing.

But there's also another reason: **if you can't present your business in a concise easy way chances are you don't have a solid plan.** When it comes down to it, the temptation to overstuff your plan is understandable but keep it simple.

So by all means go look at business plan examples, but don't over do it with unnecessary information.

Research:

When compiling your business plan, you need to compile data on two main topics.

1. The geographic area you plan to open your shop. This should include population statistics, age demographics, and income.

   This will allow you to get better insight on the size of your potential customer base. It definitely helps you focus on how to best approach building awareness for your shop.

You can also research data on smoking statistics in your state and city.

For general population information you can use the U.S. census beareus website here: https://www.census.gov/

For smoker related data check out the CDC's website

http://www.cdc.gov/tobacco/data_statistics/state_data/index.htm

2. The second kind of Data you will need to research is on the Vapor industry itself. Now there really is no organization that's compiling research on the vapor industry especially vape shops.

   Most the data and industry analysis that exists has to do with electronic cigarette sales so its difficult to get a precise idea. But in the industry section I covered some of the most important statistics. At the end of this book I've listed those facts again, along with some overall smoking facts for your convenience.

   Note: Keep in mind the industry statistics for Vaping are not exact, they're educated estimations based on limited Data.

Don't get stuck in analysis paralysis, that's when you spend way too much time researching and planning. Again these statistics are just meant to give you a better idea of your opportunity and how to reach customers.

Cost/Budgeting:

Now the truth is, and this is out of experience. Whatever your budget is, whatever you think it's going to cost to open your store. In the end it's going to definitely cost more. This is my observation not just in opening vape shops but in all the businesses I've been involved in. No matter what; its going to cost more than you thought, but that isn't what's important.

What's important is that it doesn't end up costing **A LOT** more. Its one thing to go over budget by $1,000, its completely different if you find you miscalculated and need an extra $5,000 you don't have when you've already signed a lease.

The goal of estimating your start up cost is to avoid that disaster, and let me tell you that is exactly what happened to me with my first store, and I was very lucky that I was able to fix the problem.

By the end of reading this book, you'll be able to forecast a clear idea on how much money you're going to need. Along with how to budget it. But for now lets focus on how to organize it into your business plan.

You are going to come up with an overall cost, that's the big number, that's the amount needed total. With that number you can budget for different expenses. The big number is important, but you need to be very organized and smart when you budget how much you will allocate to the different items you need to purchase.

The easiest way to organize is as follows:

Merchandise:

Most your cost will go towards this, we'll go over the best approach for deciding what to buy and in what quantities later.

Fixtures:

Everything for the store itself, furniture, displays etc.

Administrative:

Cost for all necessary permits, licenses, insurance, and bookkeeping

Marketing:

Cost to design your logo, business cards, advertising etc.

Labor:

How much will you pay your staff? If your owner operated, how much salary?

Misc.:

All the little overlooked costs like paint, or all those coffee runs

Like I said whatever you think you're going to spend, chances are you'll have to spend more. But allocating and budgeting allows you to have a blueprint to know just how much you can afford to spend on what.

Store Concept:

This is the fun part, how will your store look? What will the design be? Do you want it to be modern and trendy? Rustic and classic?

Aesthetics aside, store concept is more than the ambience. What will your main focus be? For example: Are you going to be oriented more towards drippers? Great, you'll need a build area in your store then. Do you want to have a lounge area? Do you plan to sell beverages? Apparel? These all incorporate into your store concept. The more detail the better, if you plan to add something later that's fine mention it now so you can incorporate it into your plan.

Business Structure:

It's critical to your business that you have a clearly set business structure. If you ignore it, you're seriously putting yourself at risk for a wide range of problems down the line.

Lets go over the most common business structures, but if this is the first time opening a business, or you're not quite sure what's the right choice for you, I strongly suggest consulting an attorney. Yes they cost a ridiculous amount, but it's worth it compared to how much it could cost you later if something goes wrong.

Various business structure options:

Sole proprietorship:

A sole proprietorship is when you have no other partners, and plan to operate your shop yourself. Now it may sound appealing to fully be in control, but I advise against a sole proprietorship for this kind of business. The main reason being that as a sole proprietor you are held directly liable for any and all things.

Anything that goes wrong, its your head. More so, for our industry, still being in its relative infancy it wouldn't be wise. We don't know what the long term research will show about vaping, and we don't know what kind of regulations will be passed. To protect yourself and your store, I would avoid sole proprietorships. It might sound like common sense, but there's already so many small shops owned by an individual or by couples. You might get a tax break or two, but it's just not worth the risk

General partnership:

Most vape shops tend to have more than one owner. In fact one of the appeals of opening a store is the idea of partnering with your friends who also love vaping. It sounds great on paper; you get to work with your friends, or significant other in an awesome business. I hear "My friends and I want to open a vape shop" quite a lot.

Now by all means go in it with your loved ones, I know there's a huge stigma attached to working with friends or family. But in truth and out of experience it can work. But a general partnership is still risky, you may not be solely responsible but you and your partners are still going to be held liable. Also in the event things do go south with your partner, they're much trickier to resolve.

<u>Corporations and LLC's</u>

If you haven't guessed by now, I am definitely in favor of structuring your business as a Corporation or LLC (limited liability company).

To put it simply, it's just a lot smarter...

Number one; it provides a more organized structure, you can scale it up, and most importantly it greatly reduces your liabilities. Both a corporation and an LLC have their pro's and cons, so decide what is right for you. But the most important thing is that they take away your personal liability. Legally speaking a corporation or LLC incurs the risk and obligations for your business.

That's a very simplified break down, and the rules vary state by state regarding how to start and operate either. So again either consult an attorney, or someone who has experience starting businesses.

Both a Corporation and LLC serve many of the same functions. Their difference comes into play in regards to how they're taxed and viewed legally.

They differ in the following key ways:

LLC's protect a business owner from personal liability. Owners are viewed as members of the LLC but the LLC takes on any risk such as a lawsuit, while the "members" personal assets remain separate. The LLC itself is not taxed instead they have "pass through tax" which means members are taxed through their own personal tax returns.

A corporation provides the same level of protection, but the corporation itself must also pay a tax. On top of your own income tax, otherwise known as "double taxation".

Now you may be thinking, ok well how is that any kind of debate, LLC sounds better. But there's one big advantage corporations have, they can sell stock in the corporation in the form of shares. Meaning a corporation can raise money from investors much easier, not to mention it's a more appealing form of investment for would be investors. Because they can also cash out their ownership shares and its easier to buy a partner out.

Again this is a personal decision, based on how you plan to finance your store, and also if you plan to expand it. Do you plan to open more stores in the future? Plan to launch your own line of e-liquids? Do you plan to bring in investors? Again this is why a plan is so important.

Personally I prefer the structure of a corporation, yeah extra taxes are no fun, but it allows for more flexibility in my opinion.

If you feel that a corporation is just not necessary by all means go with an LLC. Just as long as you don't take on the personal risk of a sole proprietorship or general partnership. Trust me on this one, you'll be glad that you did.

Chapter 3:
Create Your Brand

Your name Your Image:

Now for a very fun part, you obviously need a name for your shop, and along with that name some kind of "brand identity". This includes logos, and other design work to distinguish your shop from others.

Names are tricky, there is really no set rule for naming a business. Some of the most random names have become the largest most recognized brands in the world. "Google" for example. Also a name doesn't have to describe your business in any way shape or form, "Apple" is the best example. It is the largest company in the world, it makes electronics, but it's named after a fruit.

I will say, in my observation vape shops aren't exactly original or unique in the names they come up with. For every shop that has a unique name, there's 10 shops with a generic name like "E-cig World"(no offense if that's your business name).

As much as I like to poke fun at it, I will also admit it doesn't really seem to impact results that much. Perhaps because the vape industry is just beginning, but also mainly because you're a physical brick and mortar store, so you are only really targeting a set area.

I will say that E-liquid companies do a better job at coming up with unique names for their brand. Don't stress yourself too much on coming up with a unique or original name. If the spark of inspiration hits you then fantastic, go with it. But your aim should be to come up with a name that distinguishes you from any nearby stores. It's better to have a name that's easy to remember, than a name that's overly complicated.

Naming your business is personal, and one of the funnest parts of planning your shop. Everyone will have their opinions. But what matters is how **you** feel about it, and those involved. With that said, while I can't come up with your business name for you, I can offer these guidelines to serve as rules of thumb.

1. Don't use a name with e-cig in it. This is partly my personal opinion, but it's totally over used and beating a dead horse at this point. It also sends the wrong message, because you will automatically be associated with cigarettes and the stigma attached to it. Furthermore don't use a name that relates to smoking, it just has too much negative association.

    I'd avoid the word cig or cigarette used in any way shape or form. Also you're not selling e-cigs, as we discussed earlier, you're selling vapor products. Leave the e-cigs for 7-11 you want to convey that you're a vapor specialty store.

2. Make sure it's a name you don't just like today, but that you'll like next year. I made this mistake starting out, and I literally get paid to come up with names and branding ideas, so it can happen to anyone.

    I named my first shop "3 Kings Vapor"

    Why? Because, it was 3 of us starting as owners, and because it sounded unique at the time. But I ended up changing it to Vapeology. Because after awhile I realized something ...

    3 Kings was not a "brand" it sounded kind of silly. Also aside from sounding silly, it was kind of arrogant. Customers would regularly ask "so are you guys the kings of vapor". I just didn't like the name, so I changed it, and

while it didn't create a big problem, it still looked funny and was confusing. Having to send emails to our customers explaining the name change, and reminding customers we were changing the name. Not to mention the cost of new signs, even Facebook made us wait weeks to approve the name change!

Moral of the story is, make sure it's a name you love and will keep.

3. Don't try too hard, if you can't think of a unique name don't try and overcompensate and make up for it by getting tricky. Sure a generic name isn't unique, but its better than calling your shop something like

"Vaypeure Boutique" (again no offense to any shop with that name). As mentioned before, if it's not unique, at least make it simple and easy to remember.

Logo:

Deciding on how to design your logo is another personal choice. For logo, sky is really the limit. Design trends are constantly changing and each designer is different. If you don't have a graphic designer, either find one local or if you want variety try out 99designs.

There are so many options when it comes to a logo, and the smallest change can alter its entire look or feel. Also there's no set rule, It can be intricate or it can be simple and minimalist.

What I do suggest is coming up with a base foundation for it and layer on top of that. For example a basic foundation can be deciding will your logo be typography only? Or will it include some kind of image?

Then build on top of that foundation.

I do suggest not going too overboard. Yes a logo can be intricate and ornate but if people can't read what your business name is, then what's the point?

If you don't have a graphic designer check out the following website sites:

www.99designs.com
www. upwork.com.

Both platforms allow you to post open job bids for talented graphic designers who will work with you to turn your ideas into a complete finalized logo.

Pro Tip: Don't do the logo yourself, unless you actually have graphic design training. You can have the most amazing name in the world, but if it has a low quality cheap looking logo you're screwing yourself. Its a terrible sight to see a business use a poorly designed logo. Your logo is the image people will associate your business with, you don't want to cut corners in this area.

It may cost money, but a well designed logo is worth the price when compared to how much business you could lose by looking unattractive to people.

Marketing Strategy:

So you know what kind of business you want to open, you have a great idea in your head of what your vavapepor shop will look like. You're excited to make your vision a reality, you daydream and imagine having it open. How satisfying it'll feel to unlock the doors to your vape shop every morning...

not to mention all the perks of owning a vapor shop, unlimited e-liquid and products at your fingertips. Sounds great doesn't it? And trust me it is!

But before you go off daydreaming further I have a very important question...

How are you going to get customers in your door? How are you going to get people to come in?

If you think that by building it they will come, you are sadly mistaken. You have to consistently put your energy and effort towards getting customers through your door.

Vape shops are by nature a destination business. While location certainly can help, and being in a high traffic space boasts visibility. The bulk of your customers will result in people purposely looking up a vape shop. This and also word of mouth.

Taking into consideration the growth of our industry, by now many cities and towns have an existing and thriving vaper community.

How you market your business will directly determine whether you succeed or fail, nothing else matters in contrast. **Your marketing will determine how quickly you grow, and how much your store will earn in sales.**

So needless to say if you take away just one thing from this entire book, it should be the belief that nothing matters more than marketing.

Your marketing plan should answer one crucial question:

How will you get customers?

That answer will connect with your sales strategy which answers the second question:

Once you get people through your door, how will you get them to buy something.

Your mission is to drive traffic into your door, and that will require a combination of activities. The mistake most business owners make, especially first time entrepreneurs is that they think there's a one step solution that will cover all of their marketing. The analogy I like to use to explain how to effectively market your business starts with a question:

Can you build a house using just a hammer?

No you can't can you?

To build a house how many tools do you need? A whole lot of tools and materials right? Same rule applies to marketing, your house is your business, and to build it you're going to need a lot of tools.

Your marketing plan should be comprised of 4 primary "channels" what a channel means is basically an individual leg of your marketing strategy that all connect to the same goal: **Getting customers into your door**.

<u>The four primary channels you should implement to create a comprehensive marketing strategy are as follow:</u>

1. Promotions:

    Special sales, deals and other incentives

2. Advertising:

    Good old fashioned traditional advertising, such as flyers and other marketing materials

3. Social Media/Internet:

    To put it simply, no business can succeed in today's day and age without a solid social media marketing strategy

4. Events: vape shops are more than retail locations; they are a destination for the local vaper community.

Do not skip the marketing chapter, read it, then read it again and have all your partners read it as well. <u>Marketing will make or break your business.</u>

If you feel like you're not up to putting in the effort needed to market your business, don't stress. I strongly encourage hiring a marketing specialist to help your business or making sure one of your staff is capable of it.

The mistake most vape shops make is they don't have a designated marketing director. Now don't get me wrong, based on sheer location and demand you can definitely get some profitable results. But the point is you can't rely on that alone, more importantly customer awareness is crucial.

Location:

Now obviously before you can open a vape shop, you need a location. But don't worry if you don't have a specific one just yet. You should definitely be searching for one actively though, because there's no guarantee you'll find one quickly.

More so even if you do find a desirable location that's within your budget you, may not be able to get it because the owner may not be open to the idea of a vape shop (trust me it happens). There have been a number of amazing locations where I wanted to open a store, but the owner of the space was not open to it.

If you have a location you are actively considering, or about to finalize the lease for, then take some photos and take measurements so you can create a floor plan and layout for how your shop will look.

If you don't have a location yet then simply list some key criteria you're looking for such as size, and potential layout concepts.

SWOT analysis:

SWOT analysis is a very helpful tool that will help create an overview of your business and your prospects for success:

S.W.O.T. stands for strengths, weaknesses, opportunities and threats.

Together they comprise a comprehensive evaluation for your business and provide an analysis providing useful guidance and direction.

So how do you do one? And what do you write for each topic?

Strengths:

List the things you're good at, and have experience in. Are there any specific and unique skills you or your team possess?

Do you have a background in something that can help? Ex: your partner has a marketing or retail background

Also factors such as your location, or resources at your disposal can be considered a strength. List any competitive advantages like superior pricing to other nearby stores or access to specific products others don't have.

You're strengths should outline all the reasons why you're confident you will succeed and all the reasons why your vape shop will be profitable.

Weaknesses:

It's important to be honest when evaluating your weaknesses, honest with yourself and honest with any potential investors.

This is the section to list areas you need to improve on, skills and knowledge you need to acquire. Lack of experience in running a retail business, or lack of knowledge in social media marketing etc. It's important to mention things that limit your operational ability, for example limited capital, poor credit.

It's no fun thinking negative, and while a key principle for success as an entrepreneur is an optimistic attitude, it's also foolish to try and ignore potential problems and areas you need to improve on. But don't get too down on yourself, the purpose of this analysis is to evaluate then develop strategy on the solutions to improve your weaknesses.

Opportunities:

This is where you can have a little fun and daydream on all the great things you can potentially accomplish. The vapor industry overall is one huge opportunity so you won't have too much difficulty in coming up with big picture ideas. Are there no vapor shops in your city? Do you think you can expand quickly and build a chain of stores? How about launching an e-liquid line? These are all opportunities.

Also, if there are already existing shops in your area, that don't seem to be doing a good job, have poor customer service or don't offer the products you plan to carry be sure to list those too.

Threats:

What are some threats to your business? Other shops is an obvious one, be sure to research how many vape shops are within a 30 mile radius of where you plan to open yours.

Don't neglect to include smoke shops, many people who aren't knowledgeable abouting vaping still buy products from smoke shops. Also a major threat to just about everyone in the industry right now is government regulation which could greatly impact everything involved with vaping. But aside from federal regulations another threat to consider is if your state or city is planning to ban e-cig/vapor product sales. These are all threats you should incorporate into your SWOT analysis.

Operational Costs:

How much will your business cost to operate monthly? It might be difficult to know exactly to the dollar but you can definitely come up with a basic estimate. If you don't have a location in mind take the average cost for a space the size you're looking for in your area.

How many employees will you need? How much do you plan to pay staff? Will you be compensating them hourly or on a set salary?

Also, how much do you plan to pay yourself for that matter?

What are the costs of goods? Taxes? What about utilities? I know lots of questions to answer, but you **need** to factor in as much as you possibly can into coming up with your operational cost estimates.

Revenue Model:

How will your business make money? Ok obviously you're a vape store, you sell vapor products. But you can make money in other ways. Services like building can definitely be a side moneymaker, along with selling apparel. I've seen some stores even offer a full café or juice bar. Also if you plan to have a lounge component to your store, you can charge a membership fee, you can rent vapes for customers.

You can make money from raffles during events for giveaways. You can host private parties and ofcourse there is e-commerce. There's numerous ways to make revenue from more than just selling vapes, brainstorm and list them all.

Projections:

How much money do you project your business to make in sales? What do you estimate will be your gross revenue? And from that what will be your net profit?

Obviously you can't give an exact answer for this but hence the title "projections" This should be a combination of what you THINK you can make, and what you HOPE to make. Or in other words, come up with a conservative number on estimated sales, but also come up with a benchmark target of your ideal number.

This can be categorized quarterly, every 6 months, annually. The easiest way is to come up with a monthly amount and multiply that for that year.

Also be sure to include projected growth, you obviously want your business to grow.

A word of advice in determining you projected monthly earnings, its always best to under promise and over deliver. Its easy to see dollar signs and get a little ahead of ourselves imagining how your store can make $50,000 a month. By all means aim for that, because it absolutely is possible, but I don't advise anticipating that for your sales goal in your second month of operation.

Return on investment or ROI

How long will it take you to make your money back? Whether self funded or using an investor. You need to have a projected time frame of how long it will take your business to recoup the initial upfront starting costs. Technically your business is in debt until the starting costs are paid back, so how long do you anticipate it will take?

Again under promise, over deliver, this is especially important if you have an investor. It might sound comforting to tell them you can pay them back the first year, but there's nothing worse than a pissed off investor. Don't worry if you end up being able to recoup the initial investment to your investor the first year. I assure you they won't complain when you call to let them know.

Module 2

Chapter 4:
Realizing Your Vision

Now that we've taken a look at how to plan your shop, create your business plan etc. Its time to dive deeper into the nuts and bolts of opening and running a vape shop. The rest of this book will focus on different topics covering the key areas of focus required to make your store a success.

With that said, as I mentioned that as comprehensive this book is, it certainly doesn't mean you should stop learning. Aside from constantly increasing your knowledge base about the vapor industry as a whole, you should also put effort into improving your understanding of business overall. You're not just a Vaporpreneur, you're also an Entrepreneur, and an indispensable habit that can increase your success is learning, more specifically reading. I've included at the end of this book a list of suggested books, these books are ones I myself count as my favorites.

The remainder of this book will cover the ins and outs of running a vape shop. Read it, and be sure to take notes. While the business model is retail, our industry is unique and certain standard rules of brick and mortar retail don't apply. Your opening more than just a place to sell products. In my observation knowledge of vaping alone is not enough to run a successful store.

As much as I've talked about not getting into this industry strictly for the potential opportunity it provides as a business. The other side of that coin is not getting into this industry without operating your store as a business.

There's numerous enterprising vape enthusiasts that struggle with their shop. Who possess the genuine passion for the product. But lack the mindset of a entrepreneur. Just because you're passionate about the craft, it won't translate into a successful store.

I've seen a number of store owners who love vaping, but drop the ball in terms of customer service, or don't market adequately and they find themselves struggling. Which is even more frustrating because they truly love what they do, but they can't seem to get it right. Its all about finding that balance between the passion and love for vaping. With the focus and work ethic of an entrepreneur.

If you follow through and apply these principles to your vape shop, you will see the results you desire and achieve the level of success you want. But the key word there is **"follow through"**.

Information is useless unless it's absorbed and applied, simply reading it won't be enough, you have to actually take action on it.

Opening your vape shop.

So you've made the decision to make your dream of opening a vape shop a reality. Your ready to take the plunge, so where do you begin? How do you actually **open** your store?

Location Location, Location...

Is the old saying when it came to brick and mortar retail. Location plays a key role for your vape shop. Its Obviously important you find the right space and in the right area. But in the vapor industry, there are some very unique differences. For when it comes to your strategy in finding a retail location for your shop and what to look for.

The biggest and most important difference is that a vape shop is what can be classified as a **"destination business"**.

Meaning: it is the kind of business, that your target customer demographic will actively seek out themselves.

The opposite to this business type is "location" business, which is a business dependent on visibility in a high traffic area.

What tends to make the difference between the two is <u>the level of specialty and niche the business provides</u>. For example, lets take a common brick and mortar business.

Say you were to open a coffee shop.

If you were going to do a traditional café, that offered popular and well known items. You'd be a location business, and would want to get a space that has lots of foot traffic, perhaps near offices, etc.

But say you wanted a unique coffee shop, a place that offered very rare exotic coffees and teas. Your shop caters towards the hard core aficionados, and enthusiasts. Well then you wouldn't have to be so heavily reliant on foot traffic because you're targeting a specific audience. You wouldn't have to rely so much on high visibility instead targeted marketing and word of mouth.

Neither location or destination business is necessarily better than the other, They both have advantages and disadvantages. Its simply just a way to identify your marketing needs.

A vape shop has the advantage of not being reliant on high visibility because vapers will seek your shop out. Now to clarify that's not to say being in a high traffic location doesn't help, it can make a huge difference. But you don't have to depend on foot traffic alone is the point. A destination business differentiates on its niche products and services, and although vaping is a fast growing industry, a vape shop is still a specialty store.

If you think about it, being a specialty store is a very good thing. As far as our industry is concerned. Not only because you have a niche target audience to market to. But because that gives your shop a way to differentiate from other businesses that sell vapor products.

Go into any smoke shop, convenience store, gas stations, even big retailers like Wal Mart. They're selling e-cigs and ego style vape pens, not to mention e-liquids.

Obviously they're not retailing high quality products, and their liquids are usually disgusting. But stop thinking from the perspective of a vaper for a moment and think from the perspective of a beginner who knows nothing whatsoever. They don't know any better and they don't know the difference.

By positioning yourself as a "specialty" shop that's only purpose is to provide vapor related products and services you immediately become the expert. People might still unknowingly buy a starter kit from one of the many opportunistic smoke shops pushing generic no name ego pens that die in a month. But they're going to come to you when their tank isn't working and the unknowledgeable cashier at the smoke shop or convenience store can't help them. Personally I've gotten so many walk ins from people who had that exact experience that I just described.

Politics:

So, you're ready to go? Ready to go find your future vape shop? Are you busy looking up locations online and drawing up floor plans?

NOT SO FAST

There's one very crucial important step we have to take care of first:

Getting permission from the city you plan to open in.

Regulation of the vapor industry much like the vape industry itself is severely fragmented. At the time of writing this there is no federal ruling yet, and few states have installed laws to govern it. Regulation for vape shops at the current time mostly falls within the city government level. Except for states where they have passed some form of regulation.

Cities and counties themselves are coming up with their o guidelines on what is permitted. Some communities outright ban it; some are open to it, while others are still trying to figure out just what to do. Overall the government state and federal are trying to figure out what to do.

Some lawmakers are completely ignorant to what vaping is and the tremendous health impact it can have. While others are taking the time to be open minded and learn. It is for certain some regulations will be created, the industry has gotten far too big to be left ignored. How harsh those regulations are is yet to be seen.

In my experience,most cities are downright confused on what to do and severely misinformed. From their perspective, we're not selling tobacco, yet our products contain nicotine. Fortunately some forward thinking cities are putting in the time to learn and come up with a balanced policy towards vape shops, while some continue to be ignorant and outright ban us.

Every city is different in the procedures requires to get permission to operate a shop. I suggest you choose a day to visit your local city planning department, they're the ones that will be able to educate you on what's required.

If there are already existing stores in the city you want to open in, that's a good sign since it's allowed.

The best-case scenario is that you'll simply need to get a business permit from the city and you're good to go. A less favorable possibility will be that you will have to file for a "special use permit".

This is a permit that grants specific businesses with less common operations the ability to operate. The reason this is less favorable is because not only is it more expensive, but you'll have to wait for it to be reviewed by your cities planning council.

If that is the case don't be discouraged, there is one benefit in that at least your store will be protected from future laws your local government decides on.

You'll need to present a concise plan for your store, including floor plans, and a summary of operation. Luckily a vape shop doesn't require too much construction aside from cosmetics, so the maps etc. are easy to create.

If you follow vaping news, every week it seems like another community is moving to ban vaping as are states. I know from personal experience, as I am actively involved in advocacy. Its pretty much daily that my writing team and I cover something related to impending regulations for Vape About It.

The FDA is currently working on creating rules and guidelines for operation. Its important to keep in mind FDA regulations will have a bigger effect on e-liquid production than retail. But in the end, everything in our industry is interconnected.

As mentioned it's a given that sooner or later there will be some form of a wide spread ruling for our industry. But I am optimistic that while it may make things more difficult, the industry will prevail and continue to grow.

Vaping is here to stay, the writings on the wall, I think even the most staunch opponent of our industry is aware of that fact. In the future nobody will smoke, people will vape.

With that said, I suggest you do your best to maintain an open line of communication with your city planning department. As a store owner you have the unique opportunity to help educate them on the benefits of vaping and how it can make a positive impact on your community.

Finding the right location:

My personal opinion based on my experience in choosing locations is this:

Regardless of where you end up, **you can make it work**.

I opened my first shop in a very high end outdoor shopping mall, with heavy foot traffic. When I say high end I mean it, my neighbors were Nordstrom and Neiman Marcus. Obviously sales grew quickly from the start in a location like that. My other stores were in similar, high traffic shopping centers.

I opened my most recent store in an industrial area where our neighbors are a medical product supplier. Now full disclosure it is more than just a store it's my corporate headquarters for Vape About It, Vaporpreneur and my other ventures. It houses our offices, but we also built out a 1,000 sq. foot store front open to customers in the area.

The results were interesting, no we didn't grow as quickly, and it took way more effort in marketing. But within two months sales were similar to our more high traffic locations.

Beginning the process to scouting locations can be tedious, but consistency and follow through is key. First and foremost as mentioned <u>have a basic idea in mind on what you're looking for, but also be flexible.</u>

As we covered vape shops are a destination business, which opens the field of options a bit for you. Aim for a space at a shopping center if you'd like. But what if you're on a tight budget and don't want to risk being obligated to paying the higher rent that's demanded from a location like that?

There are plenty of great locations in industrial areas and office parks. I've seen a number of successful stores in areas like that. Not only are you saving money every month, and lowering your overhead. Your also probably getting more bang for your buck with a larger space.

Which brings me to the next important decision in choosing a location:

How large of a shop do I need?

The question of how big or how small a shop should be is an interesting one. Truthfully there really is no set answer. You can make it work regardless of size. That's one of the great things about a vape shop, flexibility and options when it comes to space.

I've seen some really large shops, with huge tasting bars that can accommodate lots of people. Along with shops that have an entire lounge area built in.

I've also seen really small shops be successful as well as pop up shops. Technically you don't even need a whole shop, I know someone who has just one counter inside a barbershop and he makes a killing every month.

The decision on the size of your store should be determined based on your desired concept. Really what it comes down to is do you want to do just retail, or do you envision a lounge like atmosphere for customers?

If you want to do a lounge concept, then you should look for a space that is

Around 800 sq feet or larger. If you want to do strictly retail then you can easily make a store around 600 sq feet work perfectly to suit your needs.

Most retail spaces are larger, so don't worry if you have some extra space.

Now those are just rough guidelines to keep in mind on what to look for. Again theres no actual answer. Cost is also an important factor in your decision of course.

But overall I will say its better to go with a place that's a little bigger for your needs, than smaller. Worst case if you have a little bigger place you can have more room for stock, or a back office etc.

Its better to go bigger than smaller because customers rarely complain that a store space is too big, but they will definitely complain if your space is cramped and small.

How to scout properties:

Ok so you've scoured all the property listings online, and found a few great locations your excited about. You've driven by them, scoped out the area, and everything looks great.

First and foremost your going to need to contact agent or owner of the property. If you speak to an agent a very important thing to ask is to verify with the property owner that they're ok with the proposed use of a vapor shop. If you speak with the owner directly it provides you with the opportunity to confirm with them directly.

Trust me when I say this, not everyone is going to go for the idea. I've lost out on more than a few amazing locations because the owner of the property wasn't open to the idea. Unfortunately, people associate our industry with smoking, and lack of education and fear drives ignorance. There's always a chance your proposed shop will get rejected. In case it happens, don't get stressed, I know it might be frustrating especially if the location was ideal.

But don't worry there's a great location waiting for you. More so its important to have a land lord who's pro vaping rather than one who's unsure or against it. Its much better to work with an owner that's open minded and supportive.

When viewing the property

Obviously you should ask if there is anything major that needs to be repaired or fixed with the space. But there are also some smaller easy to over look things to look for as well. For example, be sure to confirm if high speed internet is accessible at that location. Sounds like a given but I recall my second shop we discovered in fact it wasn't. Well not unless we wanted to spend $40,000 to run the cable to our shop. We ended up having to use a wireless hot spot, which was unreliable and would hardly work.

Luckily we were able to connect it with our register system that relied on Internet connection. Point is, that was a huge red flag that we overlooked.

Another important factor is neighbors; you should absolutely go speak with the neighbors. No exceptions, doesn't matter what kind of business your neighbor is, go introduce yourself and make sure they're ok with what you want to do. This goes back to the lack of knowledge and awareness the majority of people have towards vaping.

Most often people are really open to it, but if they're not, then you have a potential problem. At the end of the day it's the land lord's decision what kind of business can operate on their property. But that doesn't mean your neighbors can't make life difficult or sabotage you. Again I am speaking from experience. In fact, I had to close down a store I was attempting to open, losing thousands of dollars all because of the ignorance and negativity of a neighbor.

Sabotage by neighbor...

I grabbed coffee with a friend one day and he told me to meet him in this new shopping center that was just opening in the town he had just moved too. This town was tucked away in a beautiful area near my city of residence and was a hub of all things art, music and culture. It was the kind of place all the hip young people were flocking to.

The town was booming, growing as a tourist destination, with a flourishing local wine scene and great dining. An enterprising Entrepreneur had developed this beautiful out door shopping center. The place was perfect for a vape shop I thought. The location itself was high end, and the population was young and trendy. Not to mention there were a number of breweries, wineries and even a distillery along with tons of restaurants. I envisioned a very trendy shop/lounge concept.

Now I'm the type of person that if I decide I want to do something I move on it right away, speed of implementation. By the following week I had met with the owner of the shopping center, he loved the idea, and as it turned out his business partner also vaped.

I couldn't have been more thrilled, we already had a store in a neighboring city, and it was going to really help establish ourselves as the go to shop in the county by having two locations. Not to mention the owner was a fellow entrepreneur. We really hit it off, and his entire team were so phenomenal. In fact, I was looking at also getting office space in the area. So I could make it my new head quarters since I loved the atmosphere so much.

I signed the lease for a great 1250 sq. foot space, the rent was very affordable, and the lay out was perfect for my concept. Here's where it started to go to hell: first due to the disorganization of the city government I found out I had to apply for a permit, after they had said I didn't need any specific permit. They notified me a week later that in fact I did require a retail permit, since that specific building was zoned industrial.

Meaning in order to actually do retail I had to get a special use permit.

Now this wasn't anything new to me, I had gone through this process before for other businesses including my vape shops. As we discussed in the section regarding permits and zoning, its pretty much standard procedure.

If nothing else, it's a great way for city governments to get more money out of small business owners.

But the good news was, they had no law against vaping or any form of ordinance. Which meant I just had to go through the formalities and get a retail permit. The city planner assured me that it would be a quick process, and said its ok if I want to begin the process of moving in.

Everything was going well, and we were about a week into getting the new location set up. Our neighbors were a yoga/dance studio and an art gallery. First the Yoga studio came in to voice their concerns about our business. I politely and patiently gave them an overview of vaping, hoping a little information would help calm her opposition. I seemed to win her over, I also assured her we would keep noise down during their business hours. Our peak business hours would be well after they closed. Same thing happened with the owner of the art gallery. I did my best to act professionally with them and educate them about vaping.

They complained that children come to the dance studio, I assured them I would make it a point nobody vapes outside at any time. They complained about the vapor, which is of course ridiculous. But I assured them we'd have air movers in place and there's no way they'd be exposed to it.

I really tried to win them over and I thought I had. Until the day of the planning council meeting, which is open to the public. These people literally called every customer, friend, and family member to show up and speak out against us.

The city had received a number of letters complaining, they had a number of people go up and speak out, threatening to boycott their business if there's a vapor shop next door. You would think I was trying to open a meth lab next door. The irony is there was a marijuana dispensary literally across the street. All in all, our neighbors caused so much drama, that the city decided to reject our permit request.

Luckily the owner let me out of the lease and refunded my deposit. But I still had lost a lot of money, all because of the ignorance of my neighbors. Now do I hold a grudge? Course I do, but at the same time I should have gone over and talked to them first. Even if they were against it, at least it would have saved me lots of time and energy.

I hope my story and experience convinced you just how important of a step it is. Most likely they'll be ok with it, but it makes a great first impression and starts your relationship off on a positive note if you go over and introduce yourself that way.

Check the environment:

If your inside a shopping plaza, go talk to some of the other retail businesses and get their feed back. You may have an entirely different results but it helps to get a better perspective of the potential area. <u>When choosing a location you want to get as much information as possible.</u>

To do list:

Make a note of all the different things you'd have to fix or change at that particular location, this helps you make a better decision in choosing which space to go with when comparing the different options. What will you have to add, or change to make it how you'd like. Also I would organize it into two categories of necessity along with preference. Meaning, the floors are awful and need to get remodeled, that is a necessity that is more priority than wiring the walls for flat screen TV's for example.

Also be sure to list key variances in the different locations, for example if one has hardwood floors, if one is carpet etc.

The important question:

One key question to ask yourself when choosing a location for your vapor shop is the following: <u>Will you be happy calling this place home for the next 3-4 years?</u>

Standard leases for commercial space is usually 4 years so you have to make sure this is a place that you'll be happy coming to every day.

Now if by chance your deciding on a space that's smaller than you would like, but it's the one that's affordable then its totally fine to start small. If you plan to expand into a larger location down the line that's great, but you still need to be confident that you will be happy calling your first place home for the next few years if not longer.

The reason for this is you have to make your decision from the perspective of wanting to build a business that will last for years to come. Who knows what the Vapor industry will look like 5 years or 10 years from now. Maybe we'll go the way of most industries and large retail chains will be established. Maybe eventually everyone will be purchasing from the Internet. Who knows, you can project and forecast all you want, but you have to open your business with the mindset of being there to stay. Your focus shouldn't be wasted on expanding or how the industry will evolve. Put your mind on making your store the best shop it can be and built to last.

Agent or not to Agent:

One question I've gotten asked is whether or not to recruit an agent to help you in your location hunt. In my experience it can be a hit or miss. I had an agent who really dropped the ball on a location, the irony was the guy vaped! You would think he'd be out there working hard to close the deal, but he lagged, and hardly did much. But my current agent, he's a super hero, the man gets things done he's a veteran of the industry and he's become a great addition to my network.

They make you look more serious and professional for one. They also help navigate the process of signing the lease. They know what to look for, they can spot any fancy "legalese" written into the fine print that might not be in your favor. But most importantly they have better access to potential locations.

Do you need one? No, I didn't have one for my first shop, but it doesn't hurt. The key thing to look for is if they are actually committed to helping you or do they just want to close a deal.

Signing the lease:

So you scoured the internet, saw a number of locations and the stars aligned. You finally found your dream location and now you have to finalize the lease.

Letter of intent:

The letter of intent is a document you or your agent will prepare that officially states you'd like to become the tenant. It is not legally binding, its more of a formality. Along with an opportunity to discuss or negotiate any specifics that go into the lease

You don't always need one, if you have an agent they'll make one for you. If you're dealing directly with the owner, you most likely won't be required to make one. If that's the case its still advisable to write a formal letter.

Credit Check:

The land lord is definitely going to run a credit check and background check. If your credit isn't strong, or you haven't had the opportunity to build your credit don't worry there's ways to overcome that hurdle.

First and foremost, just be open and honest about it with the landlord, if you know your credit is weak.

You can either find a co-signer who has stronger credit. Or is a co-signer isn't an option, then offer to pay rent in advance. The 2nd option really isn't ideal, but if you have no other option then at least you won't have to worry about rent for a few months.

Regarding co-signers: Its important you communicate with your co-signer that they are partaking in shared responsibility and liability for the rent. But also that by co-signing they are not entitled to control of your business, unless otherwise agreed upon.

Negotiating Rent:

Word of advice, don't waste your energy on bargaining too much, unless you have excellent credit, a large sum of capital at your disposal and a track record of success in business. Too often first time entrepreneurs approach negotiating rent like negotiating to buy a car. It's not that kind of game, and by approaching it that way you only make yourself look like an amateur.

Leverage is key when it comes to negotiations, and you're most likely not an established company you're a start up. Unless you have a lot of credibility or you've succeeded in a different industry to prove history of success, then you won't have much leverage to negotiate with.

Now with that said, by all means try and negotiate for a lower rent, but my point is don't waste too much energy on it, don't nickel and dime it and here's why:

At the end of the day, your success and profitability isn't going to depend on getting $50 lowered from your monthly rent. If that's what your concerned about your already looking at things from a negative perspective. Your success is going to come by filling your shop with a constant stream of customers.

So as I said, by all means if there's some room there to negotiate, go for it. But leave it be if its something the land lord isn't flexible on.

Lease Terms:

Be sure to include all the additional costs you have to pay for the location. The "rent" usually includes additional costs such as triple net, or maintenance fee's.

How many years?

The length of your lease isn't just "how many years do you have the place" you also have to look at it as "how many years are you obligated to pay rent". Sounds a lot different when you look at it from that perspective doesn't it? On the low end your looking at a 3-year lease, up to around 5-6 years.

Extension option:

Some, not all land lords will also include an option to extend your lease. The great thing about an extension clause is that it gives you a sense of security. If your business succeeds you can easily extend your lease, without the added risk of beings obligated to more years.

If you don't have an extension clause, I highly suggest you ask for one, most landlords have no issue with it since it also helps them to in the long run. You have to keep in mind, commercial property is useless if its sitting there empty. A property owners priority is to always have a tenant in their space.

There is also an often overlooked benefit to a longer lease that I would like to go over. From one end, yes the length of your lease equals to an obligation to pay rent. Which can be viewed as a liability. But the length of your lease is also a factor in the valuation of your business.

Why does that come in handy?

Well let's say you want to open a second store and want to get investors, or let's say someone offers to buy your business, in either scenario the length of your lease helps determine your potential value.

You simply take your annual gross and net and multiply it by the length of your lease. This benefits you by increasing your business value which gives you more leverage in raising investment or selling.

Say for example your net profit for your store is $100,000 annually, with a gross of around $300,000. Now let's say you're seeking an investor to raise $50,000 for opening a second store.

They want 25% ownership, which is higher than your willing to give. You can use this valuation method to negotiate:

$100 k net x 3-year lease + 2 year extension
5x $100K = $500 K estimated net revenue

You could show your potential investor that their $50,000 investment is only equal to 10% of your business valuation not 25%. Leaving you with more ownership of your business, and more flexibility in the long run.

Congratulations:

Once you sign the lease, take a moment and congratulate yourself, the work is just beginning, but you've taken a huge step towards realizing your dream and achieving your goal. I congratulate you on your commitment to this industry, and welcome you to the owner's box!

Now lets roll up our sleeves because the fun is about to begin.

Chapter 5:
Final Preparation

Budgeting your store:

As we discussed, how you budget the start up costs for your store can make or break you. I know my own big mistake starting my first shop certainly put us in a bad position and I was lucky to navigate out of it.

Allocation of funds is crucial, whether you have a large amount of capital or on a shoestring budget. In fact, sometimes having a lot of money can be a bad thing. Again speaking from experience; having capital makes you more reckless.

First things first, let me answer the big question; just how much does it cost to open a vapor shop?

On the low end: 30,000

On the high end: $75,000

Now those numbers are obviously not set in stone, I know stores that spent over $60,000 just on inventory alone. There are 19234808 variables that can change those numbers quickly. But that is the **standard basic range of cost to open a store.**

Can you start with less? Sure its possible, but honestly its not worth the risk of getting into this business if you're not able to spend at least $30,000 up front.

Also its wise to have capital in reserve to cover operating costs for at least a few months, which I factor in separate from the initial $30,000.

A general break down of how much you're going to spend and on what with a bare minimum budget with an estimated rent of $2,000 a month.

$6,000: The store itself, furniture, misc. supplies, display etc

$15,000: Inventory

$1,000: Administrative cost, business permits (varies by location)

$2,000: Signage

$1,000: Marketing materials (business cards, flyers, shirts)

$4000: First months rent + deposit

$1,000: Misc. (trust me it happens)

Again to reiterate this is just a rough, estimated budget for the bare bones cost of opening a store. Realistically it will cost more, but keep in mind even if you end up spending $60,000, A vapor shop still costs far less than most businesses to start.

If you have more capital at your disposal great, you can add those led tv's and build a stylish tasting bar or whatever else you have in mind. That's the great thing about this business, you can make it work on a budget, or if you're lucky enough to have more capital, you can go bigger.

But don't go overboard:

As I said having too much capital can also be a bad thing. At the end of the day you could give your shop all the bells and whistles, have a huge selection of e-liquid and hardware. But if you don't put effort into great customer service and building a loyal customer base, none of that will matter.

My first shop was literally just down the street from the biggest vape shop in the whole county. Although we had a great location inside a high-end shopping mall, the other store was far superior. I mean we didn't even have a tasting bar, we had a tasting table!

They had way more product, more e-liquid, and they even had an entire lounge connected to the retail store.

Within 3 months we quickly became the go to shop in the area, why do you think that was?

It was because while we lacked in a lot of areas, we always went the extra mile with our customers. More importantly regardless if you were buying 1 bottle of liquid or an entire new set up, we provided the same quality service.

We also offered better pricing, which was something vapers in the area appreciated tremendously.

Nothing against the other store, they had a great staff, but while they excelled at their knowledge of vaping, we excelled at our customer service and that was our key to success.

The take away here is: nothing makes up for superior service and quality experience.

Customers will forgive you if you don't have flat screens on the wall or 120 flavors of e-liquid to choose from. But they won't forgive you if you provide crappy service. <u>Everyone likes to feel special and we vapers are some of the most discretionary shoppers aren't we?</u>

Back up funds:

You've budgeted out your money, you have $40,000 to spend and after adding everything up you can confidently open the shop with that budget. But what about leaving some money in the bank for back up?

The rule of thumb in business traditionally has been having 6 months of capital available to cover your business costs in case things are slow or you hit a bump in the road.

Personally, I've gone with only 3 months and taken the risk. It's really your call on this way. I'd be a pretty awful consultant to suggest taking the risk with no money saved up. At the same time, speaking from experience your store could quickly grow in sales within just a week.

For example, our most recent store, jumped from barely $150 a day the first two weeks to $600 a day by the end of the first month. My first shop did $9,000 its first month, and $20,000 by the second month. There is no way to tell, or evaluate how fast you'll grow. The best advice I can give is that it's really up to you, your risk. But I strongly suggest you do not try and open without at least a few months' worth of rent to cover your cost in case things start slow, Its just not worth the risk

Be sure to calculate your monthly operational cost, this doesn't mean just rent. This means every single dollar you have to pay to keep the doors open and the lights on, including labor.

From that number, divide by 30 days, to give you an estimate break even daily sales goal, along with monthly break-even point.

Services:

As I've said before, and I'll keep saying. A vapor shop is more than just a retail location. It's more than just a place to sell vapor "stuff". Your store is the point of interaction between customers and the vapor community. They come to sample liquid, get educated, and of course talk shop.

Your goal for marketing is not to "sell" but to get people in the door. <u>The more reasons they have to come into the shop, the more frequently they will buy.</u>

There are a few services I strongly suggest offering that greatly increases the frequency of your customers coming into the store.

<u>Building:</u>

If you're a vapor shop, you should without a doubt offer building as a service. First of all its one of the key ways to differentiate from smoke shops, and it's a great way to build customer loyalty. Building allows you to position your store as the go to location. Not to mention it's a great way to make some side revenue.

If you don't have space for a designated build station, don't worry, again what matters is service and quality. But if you can make the space, even a simple table to build is a great touch for your shop.

There are a few different approaches for employing builders. You and your staff should of course provide building services. But another approach is you can allow for "freelancers" to sell their services.

Look at it this way, a decent build takes time. Even a simple one, much less the more sought after "coil porn" builds.

A worst case scenario which happens often is when you're providing a customer with a build and another customer walks in. So by allowing free lancers you're freeing up your time. While still offering it as a service. You lose part of the side revenue but at the end of the day its not a substantial amount.

Another reason why allowing free lancers to feature at your shop is that they become promoters for your business. You get free marketing and promotion through their networking.

The way I usually structure compensation with freelancers is that they get to keep whatever they charge for their build, but their customers purchase their wire/cotton from us. This is also a great opportunity to upsell a customer who's there for a build to buy liquid or other products while they wait.

How much to charge for in house builds:

How we price our in house builds is as follows:

Standard dual coil: $5

"Coil art" difficult advanced builds: $8-$20 (depending on build time)

As a rule of thumb, if a customer purchases a new mod, or atomizer we offer them a complimentary build.

A word of advice, the more advanced builds are a waste of time, I wouldn't suggest offering them as a service in house because they're just so time consuming.

Set the pricing as you wish, a shop nearby mine charges much more for builds than we do. But I would advise, building is a recurring service. So I'd rather focus on building a long standing relation and charge less in order to keep my customers happy.

Other services:

Classes:

Offering classes is an additional service that kills two birds with one stone. Not only does it increase traffic, getting people into your doors. But it also adds to your customer's experience.

Vaping is something that requires knowledge and demonstration no matter what level you are. Whether its their first sub ohm kit, or their first mod, customers are going to need training.

While its true people can find any and all information online. There's literally an endless amount of tutorials and how to instructionals on YouTube. But why miss out on the opportunity to be their go to source for knowledge?

Not only do you enhance your customer service, but you're positioning yourself as the "expert" which is a crucial factor in building long term customer loyalty.

So what kind of "classes" should you offer?

You should structure your courses in 3 levels:

1. Beginner

This should be an entry level class covering vaping basics primarily focusing on ego pens, low power box mods and tanks.

Save Mods and dripping for the next level.

You should cover basic battery/tank maintenance. How to clean your tank, refill and replace coils. Its at this stage of vaping that beginners struggle the most, especially when trying to quit smoking. It is important beginners learn how to properly use their new set up.

Think about it: smoking a cigarette is such an easy process, you take one out the pack, light up and smoke. Using a box mod on the other hand can not only be frustrating but intimidating. As a shop owner it us your responsibility and duty to make sure you put effort in helping beginners learn proper operation.

2. Intermediate: Introduction to building

The next level up should introduce basic building techniques. Building isn't rocket science, but there are some very important key things people should learn in order to ensure a safe experience.

For the intro class, aside from covering actual building techniques like wrapping coils. You should also educate on safety. Sure we all love to cloud chase, but beginners need to understand proper safety when it comes to their builds. Understanding things like voltage, wattage, and the proper way to sub ohm ensures your customers safety. Also how to properly work with temperature control should also be added.

3. Advanced: Cloud Chasing

I won't get too much into my views on cloud chasing here. We'll discuss that later, but I will say I think supporting "cloud chasing" is an interesting dilemma for shop owners. From one end, vaping should be promoted as a way to quit smoking. I'll admit, I think some of the young vapers take the cloud chasing thing too far and it makes us look bad. But at the same time, I believe it's a part of the community. I believe we need to find a happy medium between enjoying the fun of vaping as a hobby. While maintaining its purpose and true mission.

With that said for the advanced course, you can have a little fun and go over the more advanced build styles. This is a good opportunity to discuss topics like regulated versus unregulated mods etc.

The great thing about our industry is that we are constantly evolving with new build techniques, new designs on products and constant advancement of the technology. Your role as a shop owner puts you at the forefront for customers to learn and discover about the latest and greatest. While the first two classes will maintain a pretty standard curriculum, the advanced level is going to always be changing with new topics.

You can treat your advanced group more like a regular meet up group, you'll get to interact with your most loyal and knowledgeable customers. Giving you a great opportunity to really build a long term relationship.

How much to charge?

For the beginner class I strongly suggest offering it for free.

For the intermediate/advanced classes, you could charge a one time $5 - $10 fee for their first attendance. Or include it free with purchase of their first set up. Which will provide added value for your customer.

The goal with classes isn't to make money, your aim should be getting people into your doors. We'll discuss other kinds of events later on, but classes are a great add on service for your shop.

Additional services:

Skies the limit on what you can offer, I've seen shops offer custom painting, and engraving. Some shops have a built in Café. But the services we went over should serve as your core, and if you have any unique ones you've thought of by all means be sure to e-mail me I'm always looking to learn new ideas.

Lay Out:

You would think deciding on a lay out for your store would be easy and fun. You couldn't be more wrong, you're in for numerous arguments with your partners, and constantly rethinking and changing your mind. But don't worry its still a lot of fun.

Lay out may not seem very important, you might think "hey I'll just put a couch in the corner and some counters in there and I'm good to go.

But your store lay out is crucial; it plays a big role in your operations.

The primary goal of any store lay out is to create customer flow. Meaning a set movement structure that determines the overall shopping experience. For example, what's the first thing you want customers to see when they walk into your store?

What way do you want to position your merchandise?

You would be surprised if I told you just how much the lay out, and customer flow of your store could influence sales. Literally it's an entire science, and large retail businesses spend huge sums of money researching it. In my opinion, its one of the most overlooked areas in our industry.

Store planners and visual merchandisers are employed by all major retailers in every industry from clothing to hardware. Now obviously those are for giant big box stores, but that doesn't mean we can't apply some of the key principles to the lay out of our humble vape shops.

For example, 90% of people will turn right upon entering a retail space, and travel counter clockwise across your sales floor.

Luckily for us, unlike most retail stores, our product categories are pretty simple. I classify product categories into **4 main groups, and one optional**.

1. Starter level, ego pens, low wattage box mods, sub ohm tanks
2. Mods and Attys
3. E-liquid
4. Accessories: drip tips, apparel etc

Optional 5th: Personal Vaporizers for dry herb and wax.

The reason why the category for cannabis related products is optional is because its really a matter of choice on your end as a shop owner. Selling vaporizers can certainly generate great sales, but some people may not agree with it, and more so it's not very crucial to your core service.

In retail lay out theory there are **four industry standard lay outs:**

Grid, Racetrack, Free Flow and Spine.

We don't need to worry about Grid or Racetrack because they're utilized by larger stores, unless you're trying to open the Costco of vaping.

Vapor stores fall into an odd hybrid of the Spine/Free Flow.

Depending on the size of your shop and if you have a lounge area or not. But for the main retail area you want to position your counters in a free flowing pattern that allows customers to easily walk around and look at merchandise.

For my shop we use a basic L-shape for our primary retail displays. With the tasting bar separate and stand-alone.

Due to the space, customers naturally turn left, therefore their shopping experience begins and moves counter clockwise. The most important thing is that we have the sales floor broken into 3 primary stations that creates a concise flow, but also allows us designate staff to each section. This especially helps at peak traffic times creating separation between product groups.

I can have someone providing samples at our tasting bar, while another team member gives a build tutorial at the build station.

You want your customer's full attention when they're in store, it also enhances their experience and perceived customer service quality. You can be the friendliest most attentive person. But your customer still may not enjoy their shopping experience simply because there was a loud group talking over next to them. These little things matter and play a big role in the overall buying experience.

I also designate a counter for accessories located right next to my register because accessories are typically lower priced and can be an impulse purchase.

The reason why its wise to separate the tasting bar is because that tends to be where the highest concentration of vaping and discussion occurs.

You don't want customers being bombarded by giant plumes of vape and loud discussions while they're browsing merchandise. By separating the Bar, it improves the customer flow for the primary retail area.

Also place the cash register at one end of the store, this will create a concise loop. While also providing a direct line of site to exit once their purchase is complete. This provides an actual "flow" from beginning to end.

Now by no means is this the only layout option, this is simply what we found to be most optimal for our space, which brings me to a key point.

You have to "fit" your lay out into your space and adapt the customer flow to compliment the size of your store.

Display:

Just like your lay out, the pattern in which you display your merchandise influences customer decisions and purchase behavior.

First let's discuss counters, since I doubt you plan to leave your merchandise laying around on tables. My preference is full vision multi level counters. But I've seen many stores use single level jewelry shop style displays.

Both can work well, I would decide based on the overall quantity of products you plan to offer. The reason I prefer Full vision counters is because I can showcase a larger selection of options. While spacing it out in a way that isn't cluttered. This Provides space for separation, and allows you to showcase higher priced items. Create differentiation between your lower priced and higher priced items.

Also as a rule of thumb, and again based off actual scientific research, lighting plays a role in purchase decisions. Customers are attracted to light, and gravitate towards it much light a moth.

For example, we have extra lighting in our display for higher priced merchandise, while leaving the display for lower priced products without it. Drawing more attention to the higher ticket items.

As I mentioned, I designate separate counters and sections for different product types. I've seen stores that don't, and personally I find that to be a mistake. I've seen stores place high priced mods in the same counter next to ego style batteries. Maybe I'm just nit picking, but it makes more sense to give every product category their own space.

Aside from the counters, you also need individual display stands for your products. <u>Do not, I repeat do not lay things down flatly or leave them flung about</u>. It makes you look sloppy and unorganized, while also lowering the perceived quality of your merchandise.

Smoke shops can get away with that because, they're smoke shops. But you own a vape store, Vaporpreneurs take pride in how they present their merchandise, remember you are also representing our industry.

High quality display stands aren't expensive, there's no excuse not to take that extra effort. Nothing turns me off more when I visit a vapor shop and I see products flung about in an unorganized careless way. Regularly check that all your products are displayed straight, and are clean.

Clearance bins:

Clearance bins can be a great way to move extra stock, and people are always looking for a bargain. I would feature no more than two bins, one for liquid one for hardware. It's the impulse buy that makes it a useful tool.

Just like the accessories counter, the key to triggering impulse buys is visibility and being within their line of site.

Tasting Bar:

Your E-liquid tasting bar is a central hub of your shop. <u>It's where customers will spend the most time. Where you will have the most face to face interactions with them</u>. It will serve as the fulcrum of your entire customer experience, so it goes without saying you need to certainly put some effort into it.

There are so many different ways to go about this, I have seen some seriously impressive tasting bars. But before you go out and spend 15k on a custom bar with specialized led lighting, and gold trim.

Truth is, aesthetics don't matter as much as the experience itself and the selection of e-liquid.

If you have the capital for it, then by all means go crazy. But the point I'm trying to make is that you don't **NEED** to. What you lack in flash, you can make up for quality service and selection.

You can have a diamond encrusted tasting bar that levitates in mid air for all I care, it means nothing if you don't provide a quality service through engaging interaction and a good selection of liquid.

This is where you're going to get the most face to face time with your customers. We're going to get into details on how to really leverage that time later in the book.

Personally I keep use a very minimalistic approach nothing fancy, just clean and simple display, because it matches my overall brand for Vapeology. Not to mention the first shop I ever opened literally had no bar and that store grossed $30 k + a month.

How to showcase e-liquid:

There are a number of various approaches to displaying and showcasing e-liquids. Go into any two stores and chances are they do it differently. The industry standard are placing bottles behind the counter on shelves. Either horizontally or vertically in columns. .

Product Over view:

The products you choose to sell, will greatly effect the response to your shop, and customer perception.

Its not so much about selling vape products, its about selling the **right** vape products. <u>Do not sacrifice quality for quantity</u>, and trust me in this industry that's definitely a mistake that is easy to make.

It's also a mistake that you can make by accident. Simply due to the fact there are so many vendors and product manufacturers to choose from. It seems like hundreds of factories in china are switching out machinery to manufacture vape related products in order to cash in on our industries growth.

Aside from not wanting to have the reputation for selling cheap crap. There's another important reason to be very picky on the products you offer, and that is<u>: poor quality products have far more problems with them</u>. Which will result in customers coming in complaining, asking for help or refunds which will end up wasting your time.

I remember first starting out, and getting in touch with various vendors and also deciding which products to carry. I literally spent almost 48 hours no sleep scouring through Ali Baba's website, requesting catalogs, pricelists etc.

The industry was a lot different then, China was the source for everything and their were very few US vendors. Now the top distributors are in the states which makes it much easier to purchase merchandise.

I put in a lot of time and research into finding out who the right vendors were, who to purchase from and who not to. I was also pretty much on my own, because it wasn't like I could go ask the local shop for advice.

"Hey so I'm opening my own shop just a few miles from yours, mind sharing with me who your vendors are?" probably wouldn't have gone over to well, So I put in the time to learn on my own.

That's why with your purchase, **I have included my preferred Vendor List.** The premium edition also includes excusive discounts that will save you thousands of dollars. Not to mention the time and money you'll save from not purchasing from the wrong vendors.

Chapter 6:
The Global Phenomena

Industry Overview:

The vapor industry has gone from small and obscure to exploding with growth in just a few short years. It is mind blowing the speed at which we've transformed into a Multi billion-dollar global industry. The last 2 years alone has seen triple digit growth, and the next 4 years promises to dwarf that.

The concept and technology of vaping as a tobacco alternative is not new. The first ever vapor device was invented in the 1960's. Herbert A. Gilbert filed a patent for the first electronic cigarette in 1963. But unfortunately Mr. Gilbert was far too ahead of his time.

There wasn't any demand for the idea considering the 1960's was an era dominated by the tobacco industry (just watch mad men).

The modern vapor technology which has lead to the industry as we know it was started by a Chinese pharmacist by the name of Hon Lik in 2003. After tragically losing his father to lung Cancer. Hon set out to create a cigarette alternative that would allow users to enjoy the experience of smoking. Without the health hazards that came with it.

The use of e-cigs grew in popularity in Europe, and gradually reached the United States by the late 2000's. The vape industry is currently in a period of rapid expansion. But with that expansion comes heavy fragmentation. There are alreadya number of large companies in the market. Early adopters such as Blu and Njoy that introduced the concept of vaping and electronic cigarettes to The United States. Who now are worth over billions of dollars, and generate millions a year in profit.

There are also countless smaller brands, such as the many e-liquid companies, and hardware manufacturers creating their own branded line of products.

The giant tobacco conglomerates are also now involved. the Lorillard group makers of Newport cigarettes purchased Blu e-cigs in 2013 for $110 million. Big names like Altria and Phillip Morris have also released their own e-cig into the market place as well. Go to any gas station or 7-11 and you'll see just how many choices there are.

The big shift:

There has been a great shift occurring in the industry over the past year. Splitting the market in two separate directions. You have e-cigs or ciga-like companies, and then you have the mod manufacturers, and numerous craft e-liquid companies.

The reason for the split is that while they both are the same thing in terms of technology, the industry side of both are two completely different worlds. The e-cig sector is dominated by larger companies all competing for the same shelf space in gas stations and convenience stores. While what I call "person vapor devices" or "pvds" products are primarily sold in vape shops and e-commerce.

The data has shown another great shift in the past year occurring. The sale of the above mentioned cigalike products are slowing rapidly as consumers opt for higher performance pvd devices, also known as open tank systems.

Starter kits now are at least an ego 650 battery and clearomizer. At the same time, the pvd market has had a literal quantum leap in performance. Sub-ohm grade tanks and high wattage devices are now the standard for even beginners.

The vape industry is small business driven and much more community oriented. To put it simply, most vape shops don't sell any e-cigs, they sell personal vapor devices.

In theory the argument could be made that they're all "e-cigs" but that's like comparing a cigarette to a high quality cigar. Most importantly, the vape industry is driven by motivated and passionate entrepreneurs. Not giant conglomerates trying to cash in as more and more people switch from smoking to vaping.

It is astonishing how much the vapor community has transformed in just the last two years. <u>We aren't just an industry, we are a community, and a full blown culture that's continuing to grow and thrive.</u>

Brick and Mortar:

The mass adoption of vaping has also lead to the rise of specialty retail shops. With an estimated 7,000-8,000 independent specialty vape shops in operation. Including multi store chains that are now moving towards franchising.

In some cities like Los Angeles, which is the undisputed hub of the vape industry. There seems to be a vape shop on every other block. While some areas are still completely undeveloped.

Even with the large quantity of stores, brick and mortar is still a very lucrative opportunity for new stores to establish themselves and grow alongside the industry as a whole. My personal projection is that the window of opportunity is going to get smaller as the already established stores grow. There will be an eventual tipping point where physical stores become too saturated, but we still have years of growth ahead of us before we reach that critical mass.

<u>Tip of the iceberg:</u>

The reason I believe that this is just the tip of the ice berg in terms of industry size is that when you compare our profits to tobacco as a whole, its barely a drop in the bucket.

The vapor industry generated $3.5 billion in 2014,

Its projected to grow to an estimated $10 Billion industry by 2010.

This includes everything from e-cigs to online e-commerce retailers.

Brick and mortar shops accounted for an estimate $900 million of that.

Now $10 billion dollars is great, but tobacco products worldwide generate $800 billion annually.

In the U.S. alone annual tobacco sales are $80 Billion and its an estimated $700 billion dollar a year global industry.

1.3 billion people smoke daily worldwide.

15 billion cigarettes are sold daily

According to the most recent cdc data there nearly 40 million smokers in the

U.S. now compare that to the estimated 4 million people that have converted to Vaping.

You see the big picture, by looking at the numbers you understand why I say this is all just the tip of the iceberg.

The question I like to ask fellow vaporpreneurs is: what do you think the industry will look like in 4 years? We've taken roughly a 1% market share of global tobacco sales, what will the industry look like when that figure is 10% market share?

Vendor/Distributor Overview:

China Manufacturers:

Usually they manufacture and assemble the products they sell themselves, or are distributors representing a number of different brands.

E-Liquid:

Producers of e-liquid, usually you'll deal with the company directly, but sometimes they have a 3rd party distributor handle their sales.

US Distributors:

Either sell their own branded products. There are a number of us distributors now as well who wholesale both U.S. and China made products.

Ali Baba:

Your Gateway to the vape industry in China.

The online directory www.AliBaba.Com is a massive success story. They are a China based company that connects manufacturers with buyers and vice versa. Started by Jack Ma in 2008, it is now a publically traded company valued in the Billions.

You can find pretty much anything you want from clothing to electronics.

Ali baba serves as the gateway to connect you with the numerous manufacturers and distributors of hardware. As mentioned I have provided you with a list of preferred vendors to purchase from. But for your own learning, I suggest browsing around after you create your account. You'll definitely be shocked to see just how much stuff is there!

I will add, personally I have built great relationships with many Chinese vendors. But stateside distributors have done a great job building a solid supply chain and I prefer purchasing from them.

When I got into this industry in 2013, It took 2 weeks between purchase to receiving products. Because they would be shipped from China. Now you can get your products within 2 days. This has greatly improved business, if you want to get into distribution then definitely purchase direct from China. But stateside distributors are the way to go for retail shops.

Our industry is developing and releasing products at a mind blowing rate. It is definitely exciting, especially when there's any kind of innovation. But it is also a never-ending challenge to stay up to date with products.

Although I will admit, some products are a little overkill, nobody needs 200 watts of performance! I mean I get the appeal, but still.

Its also challenging because you have to constantly spend time determining what new products to carry, and what to stop carrying. The industry really revolves around hype. Very few companies stay relevant for more than a few months. There is always a hype new e-liquid of the week that gets replaced by the next line with buzz the following week.

While most major industries are on a yearly cycle of new product lines, it seems like vaping is on a weekly one.

Vape products are heavily saturated and heavily fragmented. China is partially to blame, but even stateside, we're ridiculously over saturated with e-liquid. It's a good thing, and a bad thing, in the long run the market will correct itself.

The Chinese connection: a study in Supply and Demand

Our industry is rather interesting because it tends to go against the law of supply and demand. In this case, supply greatly exceeds demand yet it has yet to greatly impact the cost of goods.

Sure the newer version of a product drives the price of the prior one down, but only incrementally. More so, when you look at the actual cost of manufacturing its basically identical.

The vape industry has more of an artificially created cost in order to maintain profitability.

But its not just China:

Chinese manufacturers aren't solely to blame. Retailers are also culprits. For example, you have ego 650 kits that retail for upwards of 30 dollars, when they cost less than 4 dollars per unit.

Quality over quantity:

The biggest issue with the over saturation of products to choose from isn't the variety as much as it is the quality.

There are hundreds of the same exact model products out. How do you know which vendor to choose?

The smallest difference in the coil can make a tank flood constantly, or a battery short out and stop working after one charge.

As soon as something is developed it gets reverse engineered and reproduced by 20 other factories. Type in ego battery into Ali Baba and see how many results you get.

This oversaturation presents a huge problem, aside from having the misfortune of placing a large order of junk products.

Smoke Shops: A thorn in our side

Smoke shops or head shops are one of the biggest culprits of selling poor quality products to unsuspecting customers.

Not only do they sell junk products, but they ridiculously overcharge. To be fair, I've also seen many head shops that have upped their game considerably in the last year and have a trained staff member that is knowledgeable.

But for every shop like that there are 5 that aren't. I've lost count how many times I've had someone come into my store, needing help with the vape or mod they bought from a smoke shop.

On top of that half the time I have to break it to them that the item they bought is a knock off of something else.

Now let me clarify I'm not against smoke shops selling vape products.

If you're a smoke shop owner reading this because you're interested in adding an area to your store that sells vapes. my advice is take the time to actually learn about the industry and products or hire someone who's knowledgeable.

How to not get screwed:

If you'd like to go with vendors and distributors aside from the preferred ones, I've provided then be sure to pay attention to the following things.

1. Response of the sales rep: If the representative of the vendor provides short copied and pasted responses, or avoids questions.

2. No proof of authenticity, distributors claiming to sell the products of a known brand such as Kanger or Aspire should be able to provide you with documentation proving they have a relationship with them

3. Photos: If they're using stock photos copied from other sites thats another giveaway. Quality distributors have their own design team to take photos, not copied.

Manufacturer isn't exactly a good thing:

Also be aware of manufacturers that produce their own version of a popular product and sell it off as authentic. I don't mean companies selling clones. I mean a vendor selling the Aspire Atlantis Tank, but its really their own in house version. Even with clones, this sounds weird to say but you have countless "clones of clones".

I know how overwhelming it can be when you're just starting out, preparing to make your first large order for your shop. It's a crazy shift that occurs, going from buying 3 bottles of e-liquid a week for yourself, to ordering hundreds of bottles at once. Its exciting but overwhelming all at the same time.

Pro Tip: Take it product by product, break it into smaller parts, that allows you to think more clearly and make sure you're not going over budget.

It's your job as a store owner to stay up to date, and consistently be on the look out. Also customer feedback is also useful, I was surprised to discover that the top selling products in one city, didn't sell so well in another. We're talking locations only 45 minutes apart. So paying attention to your customer's suggestions is useful.

At the same time, don't over extend yourself and try to offer too much. We're going to get into how to purchase and organize your purchasing cycle, but first let's have a quick overview of e-liquid.

E-liquid:

At the time of writing this, there is an estimated 5000 different flavor choices for e-liquids, and new ones being added daily. Along with thousands of e-liquid companies.

e-liquid is the lifeblood of your vape shop, its what people come in for atleast once a week, its what people buy the most of. **Vape shops makes their money on e-liquid, no ifs ands and buts.**

Your selection of e-liquid will make or break your business, it might be what has the smallest margin, yet generates the most sales.

The e-liquid sector of the vaping industry is saturated far more than the hardware side. That's a good thing and a bad thing depending on your point of view.

e-liquid brands are thriving new businesses providing huge opportunities to vaporpreneurs. They're creating financial success, along with jobs in communities around the country.

The thing that I find most exciting is the fact that since we're still in the infancy of this industry. E-liquid companies are uniquely positioned to grow exponentially over the upcoming years as the market doubles, triples etc.

E-liquid is the lifeblood of not just your business, but vaping in general. Just like a car is useless without oil, a vapor device is useless without liquid.

People love the variety e-liquid offers, half the fun of vaping is trying out new flavors and discovering new tastes.

On the flip side, there is a major con to the numerous pro's, and that is: the overall saturation of the market makes it difficult to successfully establish a brand. While also making it difficult for you as a store owner to choose just which flavors and brands to carry.

E-liquids are classified by far more than just flavor and taste; there are a number of different categories used to organize different liquids.

Nicotine:

One of the things that I find so frustrating is that whenever the media covers anything relating to vaping, they tend to leave out one crucial fact. That you can adjust the level of nicotine you vape.

That's one of the cornerstone benefits of vaping as an alternative to smoking, you can gradually lower your nicotine usage and dependency. Unfortunately, the media seems to have an ulterior motive and wants to villainize our industry, but I digress.

The industry standard nicotine concentration is:

24 mg
18 mg
12 mg
6 mg
3 mg
0 mg

Some brands used to offer 36 believe it or now, which was likely to cause you to pass out. Some brands try to differentiate by offering amounts in 4 or 8 mg's etc.

In between 2014 and 2015 the majority of most brands adopted 3 mg's nicotine as an option due to customer demand. The gap between 0 and 6 was too big. People wanted the nicotine kick, but many vapers, myself included found 6 to be too strong when using a Mod.

In my opinion 3 mg is the most commonly sold strength, with 6 close behind it. 12 mg is still widely used, but 18 and 24 is rare nowadays and many brands stopped producing them altogether.

How to calculate nicotine amount:

An often asked question is just how exactly does the nicotine to liquid ratio work out.

Most people assume 6 mg's nicotine for example means there's 6 milligrams of nicotine in the bottle. But actually it's based on an entirely different measurement scale.

The amount 6 mg's of nicotine, means there are 0.6 milligrams of nicotine contained per milliliter of E-liquid. Multiply that by the amount of milliliters in your bottle to give you the true amount of nicotine.

Another question asked often is how many cigarettes is equivalent to a bottle of e-liquid. The problem is that question is impossible to calculate accurately. There are far too many variables to calculate due to wattage, e-liquid strength, etc.

The variables aside there's also one key reason you really can't calculate the number. When you switch to vaping, statistically you vape far more frequently throughout the day than smoking cigarettes.

Not to mention vapor molecules are larger than smoke, so even the amount of nicotine you can absorb is different. But for customer's sake when you do the rough math. Vaping one 15ml bottle of 12 mg's e-liquid every 5 days is about the equivalent nicotine contained in 5 packs of cigarettes AGAIN VERY ROUGH MATH

What is E-liquid made of?

E-liquid is comprised of 4 primary ingredients:

Propylene glycol
Vegetable glycerin
Nicotine
Flavor extract

Pg (Propylyne glycol) and Vg (vegetable glycerin)

Whenever an article is published asking "is vaping dangerous" they always point to the potential risks of Propylene Glycol and Vegetable Glycerin.

What they fail to mention is both are used in wide variety of products from cosmetics to food. If you ate anything that was packaged, chances are you consumed some form of pg.

Together pg and vg act as the liquid solution that bonds the flavor and nicotine together, while also providing the "liquid" that actually gets vaporized.

The viscosity of both differ, and both solutions play a role in the vaping experience.

PG is known as a humectant, which is a substance that retains moisture, hence its use in cosmetic products or food. This is why pg is known to enhance the "throat hit" and flavor of e-liquid.

VG is a much thicker solution, with a naturally sweet taste, due to its thicker viscosity vg helps increase vapor production. Which is why drippers prefer high vg e-liquids.

Which one is safer?

There is a common misconception that vg is safer than pg, or more "natural". You'll find brands promoting their e-liquid as "organic" because they use mostly vg. In truth, they're both equally safe, the reason pg gets a bad name is a higher volume of people have reported allergic reactions to products that contain pg.

Pro tip:

Higher vg liquids can be difficult for most standard sub-ohm tanks. Anything over 80/20 can clog the tank. The viscosity of the liquid won't properly soak the wick inside the coil

Pg/Vg ratio: Most standard brands feature a 60/40 blend. Some of the more craft liquid lines range around 70/30. Then you have the higher vg lines that are 80/20 plus. My e-liquid line is about 70/30 depending on the flavor concentration.

Its wise to stock a range of different options, some customers are extremely particular about the ratio, while some don't even ask. E-liquid provides so many options for variety and choice, it makes it easy to provide a lot of options.

Concerning vaporizers and cannabis:

Vaping is not just for flavored e-liquids, and nicotine delivery. Vaporizers were being utilized for cannabis long before there were vapes or mods.

Vaporizing "flower" is increasingly growing in popularity as personal vaporizers continue to advance in technology. While I'm sure there will always be purists that prefer to roll and smoke the traditional way, vaping cannabis is certainly becoming the preferred method.

As a vaporpreneur, its important to give credit to the cannabis industry. They face many of the same challenges we do. They also happen to be in a state of rapid growth just like us.

Cannabis products have long been outlawed in the U.S. with strict prohibition. In the last few years we've seen great progress in regards to legalization. A number of states such as Oregon, Colorado and Washington have passed progressive reforms to legalize the sale and consumption of it. While other states have decriminalized it or permitted medicinal use.

The vaping industry shares many parallels with cannabis. Both vaping and cannabis have the potential for making a great impact on improving people's quality of life.

Furthermore both vaping and cannabis possess multi billion dollar economic implications and opportunity. Which is why we share a common enemy.

You see in my opinion big tobacco isn't our enemy, I wouldn't call them a friend either, but they are a potential ally.

Instead <u>it is big pharma that poses the biggest threat to us.</u> Well the same argument is even more true for cannabis. Big Parma stands to lose just a drop in the bucket from vaping compared to how much it can lose to the cannabis industry.

Big tobacco is a potential ally due to the financial opportunities as well. Now I'm not saying lets all sell out to Phillip Morris. My point is simply that big pharma has a much bigger interest in hindering the growth of both Vaping and cannabis than does big tobacco.

My opinion might not sit well with people, but its true when you analyze it. Again let me be perfectly clear, I'm not saying big tobacco is good, they should never be excused for what they have done.

What I am saying is when you look at it objectively, they have the resources and power to fight for vaping, and likewise cannabis. Why would do that? Simple answer: financial gain.

You see, big tobacco has massive opportunities to gain from the rise of vaping and cannabis, while big pharma does not. Furthermore, big tobacco is quickly making inroads on catering to the vape market. Their products so far have been less than impressive. But they have the money and man power to take their time and strategize.

I'm not suggesting the industry should work with big tobacco, what I am saying is whether we like it or not, they're going to try and capitalize off vaping and cannabis. While big pharma is only going to try and stop both industries.

There is also a lot of cross over in terms of products and technology between vaping and cannabis. For example, many people are beginning to vape thc oils of varying strengths. Similar to how we integrate nicotine into our e-liquid. They use the very same tanks and batteries as we do, you wouldn't even know the difference by looking at some of the hardware.

Another new method of consumption that incorporates equipment similar to Vaping is wax. Which is a waxy/clay like substance that is highly concentrated THC. This is also known as "Dabbing" based on the process of applying the wax to a coil to be vaped. This method uses the same ego style batteries along with tanks, which utilize a unique coil system to hold the wax.

Just like with vapor hardware there is a huge variety of options out there. The China influence has flooded the industry with a wide range of products and it is saturated just the same as vape hardware.

One of the key differences between our industry and theirs is the focus on hardware, which has to do more with legal issues and distribution.

When it comes to vaping, in regards to products regulated box mods, and sub-ohm tanks, or what I consider the mass consumable sector. There are only a few leading brands such as Kanger, Aspire etc.

Sure there are various scattered lines out there offering the same product model with a different logo slapped on it. But overall there are only a handful of major players in the hardware space when compared to how many e-liquid companies there are.

E-liquid is where there is massive saturation, with thousands of lines competing for the same shelf space.

In the cannabis industry it's reversed. Due to limitations on distribution of cannabis itself. A grow op in California can't ship to a dispensary in Colorado. It is a very regionalized system which is actually a good thing keeping the financial opportunities local.

Instead there are countless brands selling vaporizers, all trying to establish brand dominance. Identical to how the e-liquid sector of our industry is.

As I mentioned earlier, the decision to offer vaporizers for the specific use of cannabis consumption is really up to you. In my experience they provide a great secondary revenue source, and a way to stay involved with an industry that's very similar to our own.

There are numerous likeminded Entrepreneurs who are working hard to build a new industry with cannabis. We're kindred spirits, except they're just a little more relaxed than we are (pun intended).

If you decide not to that's fine, but if your planning to incorporate Vaporizers lets take a quick overview of some of the choices.

Vaporizers are classified into two categories

Personal Vaporizers:

These are compact, hand held devices that can vaporize cannabis. They usually resemble a similar form factor to our ego pens.. But instead of tanks, they use chambers to hold the flower or wax.

There are two types of vaporizers, coil based and "true" vaporizers. The difference being, coils have a point of combustion. They're technically more like an electronic pipe than vaporizer.

True Vaporizers don't combust the material, they heat it to the point of vaporization. These tend to be more expensive, but customers don't mind the extra cost for the enhanced experience.

Stationary Vaporizers:

These are the giant counterparts to PV's and they aren't really discreet or portable. But they do provide a whole different level of quality and performance. They come in a wide selection of options, designs and functions with features like built in fans etc.

They have evolved greatly from the original wooden box vaporizers of years ago. They're more oriented towards the aficionados willing to make an investment in such a high end item.

Protip:

You don't need to over do it on stocking a big variety of products or choices. Leave that to head shops, online and dispensaries.

Accessories:

There is an ever increasing amount of specialized accessories for Vaping. Everything from apparel, to drip tips

The choices are endless, and we don't need to get into all of them but there are some key items you should always keep in stock. Not only does it add extra revenue, but it's a useful way to create the perception of having a wide selection of products.

Wire:

Be sure to always have wire available for customers, you can sell them by the foot, by the spool or in individual build kits made by companies that provide both wire/cotton. Never run out of wire, and always have the most popular gauges in stock.

Cleaning products:

People invest money and time into their set ups, and maintenance is crucial. Offer specialized sprays or wipes to clean.

Drip tips/caps:

As I mentioned customers love to customize, and they're always looking to make small changes to individualize. Most high end atomizers come with their own drip tips. But customers are always looking to get additional caps to customize their set up.

Cases:

What's the point of having a nice mod Mod if you don't keep it safe? Be sure to offers cases that can accommodate a wide selection of sizes. Standard holding cases, along with ones that you can attach to your belt or lanyards are an easy upsell to customers when they're purchasing new set ups.

Apparel, and everything else:

Again there's so many products available, by all means carry whatever you find interesting or customers may want. Apparel is a great way to add revenue, vapers love to represent the brands they like.

Chapter 7:
Stocking Up

How to purchase your starting inventory:

Now that we've covered a basic overview of the products you should be selling its time to go over how to set up your inventory and make your first purchases.

Your starting inventory plays a big role in setting yourself up for success. You have to walk a fine line between staying on budget. While making sure you purchase enough to accommodate a quick jump in sales.

One of the big opportunities in owning a vapor shop is that you can grow very quickly overnight. While that sounds great, it also can be a bad thing. The only thing worse than not getting customers is growing too quickly and not being able to sustain that growth.

In business, some companies fail not because they didn't do well. But because they couldn't sustain the demand and ran out of cash to fulfill purchases.

Given the nature of the Vapor industry whatever products you start with will change within the first 3-4 months of operation. With the constant pace and schedule of new products your inventory will be in a state of perpetual change.

Starting inventory is a tricky formula. When you're up and running you'll have to consistently re-order products. But its easy to organize a schedule to maintain inventory. It's the starting purchase that presents a challenge, and the most risk since you're buying it all at once.

I learned the importance of being smart about starting inventory the hard way when I opened my first store.

It definitely wasn't my first rodeo, as a business consultant, I had helped start numerous businesses, including 5 that same year. Not to mention I had started and ran my own businesses. But I still made a huge mistake in my starting inventory.

Basically half the stuff we bought was crap that nobody bought, and the other half that sold we didn't buy enough of.

This wasn't a problem the first 3-4 weeks of business, but that damn near killed us the start of the second month.

We had an overnight jump in sales more than tripling from $6,000 our first month to $21,000 our second month.

While that was a good thing, it put me in constant scramble mode to maintain our inventory. The big problem was turn around time, this is when you bought everything from China. So on average, any order would take 2 weeks to arrive.

For example, when we ran out of our most popular ego battery, it took an entire two weeks to restock. The $30,000 budget I had set for the store, turned into $50,000 as I constantly had to inject more of my own cash into the business to make purchases. By my calculation I lost somewhere around $20,000 in potential sales, from customers not buying and because I had to purchase from state side vendors with higher mark ups that cut my margins.

Not to mention the added cost of constantly having to invest more capital to correct the problem. <u>It was an endless headache, because I simply didn't plan better from the start</u>. I mean even simple things like chargers, we sold out of.

I remember one day we had to go buy an extra 20 chargers from a competing store, luckily they were understanding and cool about it but still it looked pretty bad.

We would have failed if I didn't have money to back us up. Luckily I had revenue from my other businesses, but it was definitely a stressful start. It taught me an important lesson, one that I hope other first time owners opening their shop will learn from and avoid.

So by now you should have two things ready:

A concise budget, with the total amount you can spend on merchandise

A store concept, and what you specifically want to focus on

The first thing we want to do is allocate an amount for each product category:

Beginner-intermediate level such as open tank systems, low wattage box mods, and starter kits.

High performance Mods and Attys

E-liquid

Accessories

20/60 rule:

I have a percentage split I now always apply to new stores when deciding on starting inventory:

20% Open Tank systems

20% Mods/Attys

60% E-liquid

Lets say your starting budget is $15,000. Which by the way I highly advise this to be the minimum amount you spend on your merchandise. Yes, you can make it work with less, if you recall my story, I learned the hard way what happens when you try and undercut your starting inventory.

You can of course alter this to whatever you see fit, but this formula allows you to achieve three things:

Variety of choice

Enough inventory of merchandise

Determine what products are in demand with your customers

The larger your budget the more volume you can purchase, but whether you're on a shoestring budget, or you have $100,000 to spend on merchandise. This allocation formula is the most strategic purchasing strategy based off my analysis and experience.

If you're wondering why I bundle accessories with open tank systems: that's because they tend to be low cost with a smaller mark up.

Ex: packs of wire and cotton cost $3-$4 and retail for $8. You don't need to spend a large amount in order to stock up.

E-liquid is going to be your highest volume product in terms of quantity, along with gross. But luckily you don't need to worry about turn around time in case you sell out due to shipping since liquid manufacturers are in the U.S., your purchasing schedule will differ on e-liquids than hardware.

The reason why e-liquid gets so much allocation is because that is the lifeblood of any vape shop. Customers aren't going to buy a box mod every week, but they're going to go through lots of juice.

You can get away with stocking a limited amount of hardware. But customers want variety and choice when it comes to their e-liquid.

Budget: $15,000

Open Tank: $3,000

Mods/Atomizers: $3,000

E-liquid: $9,000

Decisions Decisions: analysis paralysis when choosing what products to carry.

So how do you choose exactly what model, what color etc. when there's 30821302038023808 choices out there. Don't worry about it, as I said the process of deciding what products to sell is never ending. Your goal is quality and variety, but variety with a limit, because at the end of the day you'll never be able to sell every product that's popular.

Allow me to share my personal experience with this...

In 2013 when I opened my first shop, we sold hardware hand over fist. Those were the good old days, when vaping was just starting to get big. People were switching over to clearomizers from e-cigs and dripping was just gaining momentum.

The rise of the box mod:

That era is done, because most vapers have atleast one if not multiple set ups. Don't get me wrong, there is still a massive opportunity for beginners, as I mentioned far more people still smoke than vape. As I mentioned earlier there are about 4 million vapers in the us, and still about 40 million smokers. And depending on the time of reading this that numbe will have risen to double that, and eventually will be in the tens of millions vapers.

Its wild to see that even entry level products nowadays are far more high performance than a vision spinner and pro tank 2 which was the most sought after set up when I got started vaping..

Also this year I've noticed a reduction in the amount of hardware coming out. Sure Kanger, Joyetech and Aspire are still cranking out new products every few months. But the number of US hardware manufacturers is declining. Mainly because box mods have heavily shifted the landscape. People prefer the safety and performance of a box mod over mech mods.

The death of clones:

Remember the clone controversies of 2013 and 2014? That pretty much died in 2015 and is nonexistent in 2016, as did the preference on clones. One of the fringe benefits of box mod dominance is that they've eliminated the need for clones.

Oh sure you still have shops selling them (I don't know why). But their demand has decreased exponentially. As most products are much more affordable now. There are still a number of luxury mods and attys being released. But most customers would rather have something original and affordable than a fake of something high end.

Keep it simple:

The landscape has greatly changed in the last two years. Personally in 2013 and 2014 I would stock a large variety of choices. 15 different atomizers, 15 different mods, 20 different clearomizers etc. But we made a shift in 2015, focusing on curating a select number of products and switching them out when something new and in demand comes out.

This makes inventory management easier, and allows us to keep things fresh. For example, with sub-tanks and box mods becoming so popular, I see no need in having multiple ego batteries. I sell one basic kit as the starter level item, and that's it. I'd rather divert the money saved towards carrying more e-liquid which brings me to my next point.

E-liquid variety is what will make or break your business. Vapers want to try new flavors, all the time. They also want to try the hype juices they see on Instagram and Facebook.

We sell my own Vapeology brand e-liquid line in my shop. We price it an amazing value for a premium quality line up of flavors. 12.99 for 30 mls and we have between 20-25 flavors depending on the time of year. Yet still we aim to bring in a new line every 2 weeks. The new lines will usually sell out within a week. Why? Because vapers want to experience something new. Sure we sell a good amount of our own line too, and people have their go to flavor. But always make sure your keeping your selection fresh and updated.

So You have to make some decisions on what you want to carry and how much. s is my current break down, its my "shopping list" of merchandise I try to always keep in stock. Within the vape pen category the brands stay somewhat consistent, With Mods and Attys every month there's a new trending item.

E-Liquid:

Deciding on what brands and flavors to carry for e-liquid is fun yet challenging. The fun part is trying out all the different flavors, but that in itself can become difficult due to the huge variety of choices.

E-liquid is the most saturated sector of this industry. It has a very low barrier to entry.

You're e-liquid selection plays a big role in building your customer base. When customers find the right flavors, that keeps them coming back. But also they're always on the look out for new tastes and brands to try.

When it comes to liquid, you need to balance quality/with quantity. People that vape are concerned about the quality of the liquid, which is why you should only sell U.S. made brands.

But they also want variety of options, and the opportunity to try different flavors. Furthermore, many vapers are after the newest hype flavors they see being promoted on social media.

Every now and then you'll have a customer that only vapes a certain flavor or brand, but picky customers like that are rare. The majority love to try and sample new brands and tastes.

So first and foremost how do you find and approach e-liquid manufacturers for samples?

I'm reminded of the funny meme of a lemonade stand with the caption "I own a vape shop send me samples".

Every day liquid brands are bombarded with free sample requests. Speaking from personal experience, and from speaking to my friends who own lines. Its important to respect their position when it comes to sending samples.

They have eat the cost of those bottles when sending out samples, so showing appreciation is always a good thing.

Finding liquids is easy, you should already know of some popular brands to contact. But also social media is a great tool for finding out about new up and coming brands. One thing we do every week is find at least one new liquid lines that seem interesting, and we contact them.

When contacting them its important you come off as genuine and polite. Also include your business address, and website along with photos of your shop if possible. Even if you're still remodeling the place. This gives you credibility to the company your contacting.

Pro tip:

Although I've done some of the work for you in the preferred vendors list, I suggest you find some lines yourself, especially local ones. One of the great things about E-liquids is that in every region there's fantastic craft style producers. You can support your local vape community while also gaining an edge by offering products customers can't purchase online or from other shops.

Selecting flavors:

Selling popular sought after brands is important, but what's also crucial is variety of flavor choices.

Flavor category breakdown:

Tobacco

Mint

Dessert/Savory

Fruit

Beverage

Fruit flavors should comprise the majority of your flavor options, with desserts/savory flavors being second. These are the most popular flavor types that you will sell the most of.

How many flavors should you carry?

The minimum flavors a store should carry is 60

The maximum is 100

50 may sound like a lot, but its really not when you consider there's an estimated 5000 flavors available on the market today.

Why stop at a 100 flavors?

I know plenty of stores that offer more than 100 flavors to purchase. But there's a business reason not to over do it with choices.

The more flavors you have, the more time customers will take sampling, and the more indecisive they will be.

This is a question of turn around time, the amount of time you will have to spend with a customer as they try flavors.

Also anything over 100 is somewhat overkill, advanced long term vapers already know the kinds of flavors they like, so it makes no difference to them, and beginners will just be overwhelmed.

Pro tip:

Its better to have too many flavors than not enough

Ideal number: 60 + 5

In my experience 65 flavors is the sweet spot. This provides variety and options but isn't overwhelming. But I also introduce and test out one new line every two weeks, this allows me to offer new options and tastes to customers. This is a key technique, as I mentioned many of your regulars will want a constant stream of new flavors to try. This will always increase sales by upping foot traffic.

The +5 means I keep on average 5 new flavors in rotation at all times. While switching out old ones.

You want to keep your flavor choices fresh, and be on the look out for emerging lines and popular flavors. That's why every other week I like to test out a new line, and if its overwhelmingly popular I'll continue to carry it. This allows you to push out flavors that don't sell as well, while offering new choices.

One hit wonders:

Every few months a particular taste emerges as overwhelmingly popular; it reaches critical mass across the country/world. Which in turn influences the industry to release numerous similar variations. For example, Strawberries and Cream was massively popular for awhile, then Vanilla Custard, and now at the time of writing this doughnut flavors are all the rage.

The reason why I call them one hit wonders is because they gain massive popularity for a short period of time but eventually decline as a new flavor craze takes hold.

Then they transition into staple flavors, that are commonly featured in lines.

While this effects e-liquid makers more than store owners, you should always be on the look out of the "in" flavor, Stock it, but also keep in mind you'll eventually have to replace it with the next big thing.

Dealing with MOQ's:

When I got into this industry most e-liquid companies tended to have minimum purchase amounts. It was a bit frustrating because it would limit your budget to pick up a variety of lines.

Nowadays to remain competitive most companies don't, or they have some very reasonable ones.

Some still do require a high moq which is ridiculous in this day and age. There's some brands I refuse to carry even though they make great flavors. because I dislike how they try and push an unfair moq on you.

I completely agree that e-liquid brands should have a minimum order amount. It obviously has to be worth the effort for them and they need to make their money as well, we're all part of the same supply chain. But when you're first starting out you need to build your inventory, this requires a lot of investment and you won't know which flavors will sell until your actually open.

This is always a factor, even if you have a large customer base. For example, although we move a high amount of liquid every month, I never place a large order of e-liquid for a new line. I don't know how well it will do, and if by chance it isn't well received then I have to eat that cost.

Fortunately most brands are flexible and understanding of our position as storeowners and will work with you. On the flipside to that also be considerate of the e-liquid company as well.

Its ok if you place a small order to replace a popular seller, once you've established a working relationship. But what's not ok is if your first order you only want 15 bottles.

Quantity over Quantity:

Your goal and objective is to build your menu to at least 50 favors. The rule of quantity over quantity means you should aim to purchase quantity of liquid flavors over quantity of units. You can place more orders later as you figure out what flavors sell the best.

Wick and Wire:

This is a matter of preference, some key things to stock are:

Wire: as mentioned popular gauges, by the spool or pre-packed

Cotton: Its always a nice touch to offer individual pieces for free, unless it's a whole bag. I've seen stores that charge 0.25 cents a ball, its pointless.

Purchase schedule:

After you open up and begin operating, you'll need to figure out an organized schedule to repurchase products. I prefer a two-week cycle for both hardware, and liquid. This allows you to anticipate sales, without running the risk of selling out of key items. Or you can buy in larger amounts once a month. You have to determine that by your volume of sales.

Inventory management: Its absolutely crucial you implement an inventory management system. This not only helps simplify the time spent on tracking sales, but it also gives you useful insight into what sells the best.

Module 3:
Operating Your Store

Chapter 8:
Running Your Shop

Congratulations for making it this far!

By now you should have a clear understanding of how to take the first steps towards opening your vape shop. We've covered how to find a location, get a lease, create you lay out. We've also went over the different products you'll be selling, along with how to make your starting purchases for inventory.

Some of it may have seemed tedious, but trust me its paying attention to the tedious things that end up making a big impact. Managing inventory isn't fun, but it will make or break your profit margins.

Like I said at the beginning, owning a vape shop isn't just talking about builds and blowing clouds all day. This is a BUSINESS and the shops that succeed are the ones that treat it as such.

Everything until this point in the book has been focused on the logistics and steps to open your store. The remainder of the book will cover the ins and outs on how to actually operate and grow it.

This final module will cover everything from managing your shop day to day, along with crucial activities like marketing, sales and customer service. Now that you've learned how to start your shop its time to learn the principles that will turn it into a successful one.

While a lot of the things we've discussed so far can be altered and adapted to your budget, and preference.

The principles and concepts we're going to cover cannot. What I mean by that is, the principles of success in any business are universal. It doesn't matter the industry or the business.

There are no short cuts to success, it takes consistent diligent effort and action. You get what you put in, that's the principle of reciprocation. In business the more value you provide, the more you will succeed.

The steps you need to take to open your vape shop, you'll do once. But the following topics will be ongoing actions you take every day.

Management:

As a storeowner your going to have to wear a number of hats, successful business owners do whatever they have to do, whatever needs to get done.

Whether that's helping a customer with a build, placing orders or scrubbing the toilets. You have to be willing to step in and do whatever your store and employees or partners need.

But at the same time, you have to make sure you always refocus on your biggest job, which is to manage and grow your business.

Your attention should be focused on three key areas:

Accounting

Staff

Marketing

Accounting:

How much have you sold today? This week? This month? What's, your target sales goal for the month? What's the net profit on your sales last month?

Accounting will make or break you, the more organized you are with your books, the better. More importantly unorganized account will come kick you in the ass when its time for taxes. My suggestion is don't try and do it yourself, invest the money to have a skilled book keeper.

I admit, accounting isn't my strong suite (I pay my cfo for that) and I try and avoid advising on topics I'm not well versed on. But I will tell you the key things to focus.

Money in and money out:

Everything aside you need to know 3 important numbers.

How much your grossing, how much is your net, and what's your over head.

From those 3 metrics you can determine the health of your business.

Your first goal is simple: Break even

From there, your monthly goals are really up to you and what you aspire towards.

On the high end I can tell you most high performing shops do somewhere in the range of $40,000 to $50,000 a month. Keep in mind location, region etc play a big role in that. But that is from experience and observation the ball park range for a high performing shop.

But keep in mind if your overhead is only $4,000 a month, and your selling $20,000 in merchandise that's not a bad gig.

You should always aim to increase sales, but also retention and consistency is important as well.

Staff:

Your Team:

Nobody succeeds alone, nobody. The most well known successful Entrepreneurs Steve Jobs, Mark Cuban etc.

They succeeded because they had a hard working dedicated team behind them. Sure they were the visionaries, the leaders, but there's only so much one person can do. Whether you're starting a store with 2 partners, or you have a staff of 10 employees. Team cohesiveness is crucial.

There are 3 factors that determine a successful productive team:

1. Delegation:

You and your team no matter how small or large should have clearly defined delegated areas to focus on. Let's say you have 2 other partners, who's main focus is marketing? Who's is operations?

Delegation sets the momentum of focus. If you know your role, you know where to place your energy. Team work is not a group of people trying to do a bunch of random things at once. Successful teams work together towards a common goal in this case a successful vape shop. This is achieved by each person putting their energy into a specific area. D

Delegate tasks amongst you and your partners/employees, creating a solid structure and organized focused effort.

2. Shared Vision:

Does everyone have the same vision? The same goal?

Does everyone know what the monthly sales quota is?

Shared vision is not "we want to succeed" that's a vague broad preference. Shared vision is grossing $30,000 a month in sales, and opening a second store within a year. Having shared vision aligns your efforts into one unified direction.

3. Communication:

If anything makes or breaks a team it is communication. Poor communication equals poor team work, and poor team work equals poor results and in business that equals poor business owners.

Communication is crucial, positive or negative it doesn't matter. You have to be able to communicate with each other. Disagreements will always occur, that's a universal fact in any type of relationship whether business, family or romance.

Its how you communicate and resolve disagreements that will impact your team more than the disagreement yourself. You have to be willing to compromise and be open to seeing things from another person's perspective.

Check your ego at the door:

Whether a business partner or an employee, you should never let ego get in the way of deciding what's best for the business. I myself used to be guilty of this.

Its not a matter of who's the boss, or who's in charge. Power trips are never productive. It always results in someone feeling disrespected and upset. More so how you treat your staff and partners directly impacts team morale.

Your goal is to be a leader that others WANT to follow and listen to. Who in turn makes others feel appreciated and respected. Not someone that others HAVE to listen to because you're their boss, or business partner.

The secret to successful communication is...

Listening!

Listening to others plays a bigger role in how you communicate than what you say. You're not always right, and if you have the mindset that you are, you'll get nowhere.

Sure there might be heated discussions about key issues, especially if it's a matter you're passionate about. But its how you listen to others that will determine your effectiveness in communication. People want to feel respected and listened to. Even if you don't agree, by listening you at least can communicate WHY you think your way is better, in a calm respectful matter.

Don't be the smartest person in the room:

I have a rule that I've learned over the years. I never want to be the smartest person in the room. What that means is, I want to work with and surround myself with people that are smart, intelligent and clever. I want to work with the best people I can work with. Successful entrepreneurs are not the smartest. They're successful because they're smart enough to surround themselves with smarter people.

Your job as a business owner isn't to be the smartest person, but to be the visionary and leader who can build a team of smart people.

I'm fortunate to have an amazing team of people in my companies. I may be the one with the big ideas and strategies. But I rely on them to tweak it and improve those ideas.

Dealing with Partners:

Most vape shops have a number of co-owners, again nobody succeeds on their own. Partnerships are great, if you actually work as a team. Not if it's a constant battle for who's right, and so on. Your partnership dynamic is going to make a big impact on your business.

If you're going in it with a friend or family member, you have to both agree to keep business and personal relationship separate. Because even if things don't work out business wise you can still maintain that relationship.

I started my first shop with one of my best friends, he's like my brother. We both got into vaping together and quit smoking together. He decided after 6 months he no longer wanted to be a part of the company. While he's no longer involved, we still maintain a great friendship.

I love working with partners, I'm a firm believer in it. But its also choosing the right partners, I've made the mistake of working with the wrong people and its an unneeded headache.

I personally don't like to work with people similar to my working style, I like people to compliment areas I lack in.

For example, my partner in my food truck businesses couldn't have been more different than me. Sure we shared the same drive and motivation. But we're total opposites, and oh did we absolutely butt heads.

The guys a ball breaker, but that's what I loved about him, and I absolutely loved working with him. Together we were a force to be reckoned with, and we complimented each others strengths and weaknesses. Which is why we being so so successful.

Your partners and yourself need to be united, not divided, you have to align your personalities and ideas to fit together into one cohesive unit.

A key thing to do before you start any partnership is create an agreement between yourselves. TRUST ME, this will come in handy in the event things don't work out. It doesn't have to be an intricate contract, just lay down the foundation of what the partnership entails, who gets what and most important an outline of how you'll dissolve the partnership in case things aren't working.

Doing so will greatly reduce potential headache down the line.

Customer Service:

Marketing and advertising is what will get people into your store, customer service is what will get them coming back.

The level and quality of customer service you provide can be the difference between success and failure.

You don't want customers…

Instead your goal should be to convert people into customers and then into raving fans. Read that again, you don't want "customers" you want raving fans.

What's the difference? A customer will give you a purchase, a raving fan will give you loyalty and referrals.

If there was one area, I'd say vape shops frequently drop the ball on its in customer service. In fact, as I shared at the beginning of the book, poor customer service was one of the reasons WHY I decided to open a shop in the first place.

I think the reason is two fold: For one many shop owners may not have any experience in running a business. Many owners are first time entrepreneurs.

Also they're in areas with little competition so they can basically get away with it.

At the end of the day you can't please everyone, and in any business you're going to have difficult customers, that's just the name of the game.

But that's occasional, not the norm, its still no excuse to provide crappy service.

The difference between a sub par customer experience and a high quality customer experience comes down to a simple factor of effort. How much effort do you place in helping a customer? Are you helpful? Are you patient? Do you offer guidance? Are you attentive?

Pro tip: people like to feel special, they like to feel like a VIP

The effort you place in customers ties back into the question of passion. If you're genuinely passionate about vaping. Then you're genuinely passionate about providing a great experience to your customers. Because that passion naturally translates into how much effort you place in customers.

Put yourself in the position of a customer, when you go shopping for clothing for example. What do you prefer, a helpful attentive person that engages you, smiles, offers suggestions and is patient? Or someone that looks like they're dying a slow death from utter boredom, and looks as if you're inconveniencing them just with your presence.

Are you likely to refer a friend to go there? Even if you find what you're looking for, your experience is still going to be tainted by the crappy service. This matters exponentially more for a vape shop, because building a regular loyal customer base is crucial to your success.

The power of attentiveness:

The reality of helping customers in a vape shop is that you're going to have to be extremely patient with them. A customer will ask you question after question, and you have to be prepared for that.

They're going to want to try 25 different e-liquid flavors, hell some will want to try every flavor you have and still won't buy anything. I've actually had that happen where someone will sit for 30 minutes trying flavors only to say they don't like any, or they're waiting to get paid. You have to be attentive, patient and friendly.

My secret to success:

The one determining factor as to why I succeeded quickly when I opened my first shop was customer service. Sure we also offered lower prices than nearby stores. But the key difference was the effort we placed in the customer experience.

Whether you were buying just one bottle of e-liquid or spent hundreds of dollars for a new set up, you would get the same quality service.

That's it, no secret sauce, no special marketing techniques, just high quality service. That builds customer loyalty and trust.

Provide an experience:

To succeed long term within this industry as a brick and mortar retailer, its important you realize your goal is to do more than "sell vape stuff".

A shop is where customers come in to "experience" the vapor community.

Vapers stay in the loop of what's going on in the community through social media. But they come into stores to physically interact with it. They come into your store to touch and feel, to talk shop, discuss and learn.

The best way to accomplish the goal of providing an experience is to position yourself as the local hub for the vape community. You want to be the shop everyone goes to interact on a local level.

Vaping isn't a solo hobby, one of the reasons people convert from casual vapers into passionate aficionados is the social element it provides. Really at the root the vape community taps into a basic human need to belong and identify with a group. Vaping provides that, which in turn provides you the opportunity to help facilitate that community aspect on a local level.

Establish loyalty:

You can offer promotions, advertise non stop etc, but non of that matters as much as building customer loyalty. On average a casual vaper will go to a shop a week. But for an avid vaper its at least three times a week. Vapers usually stick to one store when they find a shop they like. Your objective is to be that shop.

You're competing with other stores, head shops, not to mention the internet. Customer loyalty is your biggest goal when it comes to customer service. Its really simple: great customer service + experience = loyalty and regular clientele.

its important you reward loyalty through special incentives and pricing for your customers along with "special treatment".

For example, something I do with my regular frequent customers: I always have them try samples of e-liquids we're testing out and ask for their feedback.

It costs us nothing, but it makes them feel special. It makes them feel VIP that we value their opinion. Another simple way to enhance customer loyalty is simply giving them an extra 10% off or a free bottle at random times. This is a discount just for them. Again your goal is to make them feel appreciated.

The power of generosity:

The mistake most retailers make is they try and "bribe" customers. Through things like reduced pricing, and special sales.

Not that you shouldn't offer deals, and special promotions. But keep in mind, although it will get a boast in sales. It will not actually create LOYALTY.

Because you're not actually showing appreciation to the customer, you're just simply trying to bribe them with a lower price. Generosity on the other hand builds strong loyalty and rapport.

It's the small things that count.

you'd be surprised but simply offering a customer a beverage while they sit and chat. Is far more effective than a sales promotion when it comes to building loyalty. The ironic thing is a loyal customer that views you as generous and appreciative. Will have no problem paying any full premium price.

Building loyalty requires the personal touch, and will make all the difference.

Pro tip: remember names, ask for customer's names, and introduce yourself, remember their name and use it. Trust me this makes a huge difference.

Take the extra step:

How do you go the "extra mile" when assisting a customer? Its all about effort. If someone walks in and asks for a particular product do you point and say its over there?

Or do you walk over to the counter and take it out so they can see it?

If someone wants to try e-liquid do you sit there and wait for them to choose flavors while looking at the menu? Or do you offer them suggestions?

Its these small extra steps that make the difference.

Always greet them at the door:

The second a customer walks in your shop, you must greet them and be attentive. Literally the difference of a few seconds can greatly impact the first impression.

I have a 2 second rule with my staff, anytime someone walks in, they must be greeted within 2 seconds.

Training your staff:

If you have employees, then its crucial you instill in them the importance of customer service. You might be willing to go the extra mile, but that's because you're the owner, its your ass on the line.

One of my biggest pet peeves is vape shops with indifferent inattentive staff.

Your staff is an extension of you, they are representing YOUR business. I don't care how knowledgeable a person is. If they don't provide great customer service, I won't hire them.

In fact, I recently let someone go because of that exact reason, he knew anything and everything there was to know about vaping. But that was his Achilles's heel. Because he acted like a snob towards customers.

If it was a casual vaper using a tank, he'd hardly lift a finger to help. Even going as far as to tell a customer his set up wasn't "real" vaping. Because he wasn't using a mod.

With more advanced vapers he'd be even worse because he was condescending towards them. After repeated attempts to train him, and warnings we had enough and let him go.

Be weary of hiring these kinds of employees. Anyone who owns a shop will regularly encounter a devoted vaper who asks for a job. There are many knowledgeable and experienced vapers who know their stuff and are genuinely passionate.

But they also have a snobby elitist attitude because of it, which will kill your business.

To put it bluntly, I certainly value the level of time and commitment put into learning vaping, and I can understand why one might develop a superiority complex.

But at the end of the day, this stuff isn't quantum physics, its learning the most basic fundamentals of electrical science.

My point is, the technical knowledge can be taught, what's far more difficult is teaching proper customer service and a cultivating the right attitude.

<u>Dealing with complaints and difficult customers:</u>

In any business, retail in particular. You're going to have difficult customers and you're going to have to deal with complaints. At the end of the day you will never be able to please everyone, but that doesn't mean you shouldn't try to.

Dealing with complaints can be difficult and annoying, believe me I know.

But you still have to provide service with a smile while doing you're best to resolve the issue.

Here's the truth of the matter, people are crazy. But you have to have thick skin and keep cool. No matter how difficult the person is.

Sometimes the problem is such an easy fix, by being patient and attentive you can easily diffuse the situation.

I recall a woman came into my shop one day and bought a starter kit, just a simple ego battery and clearomizer. Two hours later she comes storming in, furious and upset, yelling about how I sold her junk.

I apologized, and calmly told her I'd do my best to see what the issue is or replace the vape for her.

Turned out she hadn't turned it on, and obviously wasn't paying attention when I showed her how to turn it on.

Now part of me wanted to laugh and yell idiot!

But I could tell she was visibly embarrassed. I simply smiled and said, no problem happens all the time! She became a regular bringing in two of her friends to buy later that week.

But at the same time, there's always going to be rude customers who feel entitled that you can't satisfy.

On another occasion, a customer had purchased a box mod/sub-tank from me. A week later she brings it in complaining that it had stopped working.

It was visibly dented from dropping it on the ground, and the contact on the box was pushed in. A result of twisting the tank in too hard.

Basically it was user error, not defective hardware. I don't replace or refund an item because of user damage. That obviously wouldn't be good for business. I explained to her what had happened, she was furious I wouldn't just give her a new one free of charge.

I offered her a replacement at a very big discount, which she agreed with. So here I was thinking "cool problem solved, satisfied customer".

The next day she leaves an awful yelp review for my shop...

Like I said you can't please everyone.

<u>A final point on customer service:</u>

Treat your customers with appreciation, listen to them, ask for feedback. People love to feel included, Reward loyalty and always make sure you say thank you, remember their name, and most of all be grateful. We live in the thank you economy. Customers have limitless choices; they don't HAVE to shop from you. Therefore, gratitude, goes a long way.

Chapter 9:
Sales Strategies for Success

Selling to customers:

The term "selling" is usually associated with door to door sales people or car dealerships. "Selling" has a negative connotation to it, yet whats often overlooked is that virtually everything is "selling". If you disagree with me, let me put it this way:

Selling is simply the process in which you convince someone to make a decision you want them to make. If you take that definition, you can apply it universally. Which is why sales skills are so useful and important.

<u>Selling is fun:</u>

I never understood the stigma attached to selling, I love to sell, because I don't view selling as "selling" I look at it as problem solving. When I sell something, I'm solving a problem for a customer. This is universal in any business, whether you're selling consulting, or vapor products. If you "hate" to sell, if you find it difficult to talk to people, and engage with them, I strongly suggest you either partner with or hire someone who's skilled at it.

The secret to successful selling…

The most effective form of selling is, to not sell. Confused you there with that one didn't I?

Selling without selling means you shift your perspective on what it means to "sell".

You're goal isn't to "sell" a customer, its to help guide them to a decision that will solve a problem. Effective salespeople don't sell, by using high pressure tactics. They close sales because they're consistent and because they provide a solution to a problem. When we buy something, we're buying something out of a perceived need. Sure there's different factors that determine just what we specifically purchase, but at the root there is a NEED.

For example, its winter and you **NEED** a new coat for the cold weather. This is your problem; your solution is to purchase a coat. Now the style of coat, material and color, those are all factors of preference and self expression.

Let's say you have other coats but they're all worn down, and old or no longer fit. You're not looking for a coat for style, your reason is to stay warm. This is a genuine need. Or you might already have a number of really nice stylish coats, but you're bored with them. You saw a new one that you really like and you want to buy it, this is "perceived need".

Customers are looking for a solution to their problem, that problem creates either a genuine need or perceived need.

How does that apply to your vape shop?

Because the objective of your sales strategy is to position yourself as the solution to your customer's problems. People come into your store because they need help, they need help on a build, they need help selecting their first mod, they need help to get started in vaping because they're ready to quit smoking and don't know where to start.

Think about it; you can buy anything sold in a vape shop online, and for cheaper.

Why are brick and mortar shops still thriving at a time when most of retail is getting its ass kicked by Amazon and e-commerce?

Because we solve problems and provide answers. We provide solutions and guidance, that online can't. whether it's a genuine need ex: "I need to quit smoking, I'm going to try vaping, I NEED a vape pen. Or perceived need ex: "I want a better atomizer for my mod because I want to expand my collection or get better clouds"

Customers come in for guidance on decisions such as those. You're sales strategy is to guide/advise not sell.

Pro tip: When a customer walks in, 9 out of 10 times they have already made a decision to purchase. Its your job to help guide them towards specifically what they'll purchase.

Know your customers needs:

What do our customers need? What is it they're looking for?

Here's a little secret, we have a great advantage in identifying our customers needs because we've been in their exact position.

Let's identify the needs of a first time customer, a beginner who's completely new to vaping.

Think back to when you first decided to get into vaping, do you remember the first time you walked inside of a vape shop?

How did it feel and what was that experience like? Or remember the first time you went online to do research, recall how overwhelmed you felt when you saw the massive amount of information out there?

How confusing was that, spending who knows how long watching videos, or reading up on things in forums.

Can you list some core needs of that customer?

What do they want? Its not a "vape" they want guidance and answers. They could have bought a starter kit online; the reason they came into your store was to get help on which one.

Its important you consistently remind yourself to look at things from the perspective and mindset of the customer. Your job is to always strive to provide the solutions to their problems.

The structure of selling:

There's various breakdowns on the proper steps to a sale, we've taken those formats and created an effective and comprehensive way to structure your selling process when interacting with a customer.

Step 1:

Open/qualify:

Greet the customer, in a friendly warm way, and qualify them. Qualifying as applied to this system means determining their intent. I always ask something simple like "So what brings you in today".

Based on their response you can determine what they're looking for and guide them.

Lets say they respond with: "I'm looking for a new box mod"

You can then follow up their response with another question, in this case I would normally ask them what they currently use.

They respond with showing you their set up. Based off that answer I'd transition into the next step.

Step 2.

Building rapport/Gather information.

So far we've qualified our customer, we know they're looking for a new box mod, and that they currently vape. At this point you begin building rapport while doing a bit of reconnaissance to get more knowledge on your customer and their needs.

Rapport is one of the most powerful tools in selling, in short it means establishing a connection and familiarity with your customer. Rapport is the first step towards creating a long term loyal customer.

In this phase its all about creating a dialogue, and most importantly keeping the attention focused on the customer. You want to ask questions that allow you to match their needs up with a product, while also making them feel like they're being assisted and helped.

You want to ask "Open ended" questions, basically questions that require more than a yes or no answer.

While your engaging in the conversation you need to pay attention to what they're saying, its all information you can use to determine what the best option is for them.

After you've gotten what you feel is sufficient information, and have established initial rapport, its important to guide the conversation and shift into phase 3.

Phase 3. Presentation

You've determined what product is the best match for them, now its time to present it, and educate them on it.

Remember your job is to serve as an expert, they're entrusting your opinion. You want to maintain control of the experience by guiding them to purchase the right product that matches up with what they want. Your job is presenting the choices that solve their problem or meet their needs.

Don't overwhelm them with too many options, I've found limiting the decision between two choices is the most effective. Why only two? Because human beings are naturally conditioned to operating within two option decisions.

Right or left, up or down, yes or no, its conditioned into our unconscious to make decisions within that format.

As opposed to how indecisive we can be when offered multi options to choose from. Case in point how much time does it take to decide what to eat for dinner when with a group of friends?

Offer two options and always lead with the higher priced item first, and lower priced item second, then circle back to the higher priced.

Perception of value plays a big role in making decisions, and by leading off with the higher priced choice, it positions it as "better".

Closing:

After you have presented different options and answered any questions its time to close. Its important to clarify this doesn't mean rush them to buy.

You have presented the solution to their problem, its time for them to decide. This is another reason why its wise not to overwhelm a customer with too many options, they'll take longer deliberating and they will be more confused.

Closing should never be as blunt as "so you wanna buy it or what" that's how you DON'T want to close. I find what's most effective are the following two closing techniques:

Presumptive close: You assume they want to buy, and simply ask something along the lines of "should I grab these for you, or is there something else I can help you find"

Double bind close: Similar to the presumptive close, except you give them two options, lets say they're looking at two different colors "so would you like to go with the black or with the red? I have both in stock"

As you can tell both of these techniques aren't closing by force, rather guiding the customer to decide.

Upselling:

After guiding them to make their decision, you want to upsell the customer.

What upselling means is offering other products that they may want to add to their purchase.

One of the great things about vaping is that there are so many smaller items you can always upsell. A another tank, a drip tip, an atty, and of course e-liquid.

The easiest upsell is to ask if the customer would like to try e-liquid, unless ofcourse they came in to buy e-liquid. Don't miss the opportunity to ask if they want to try e-liquids, that is this industries most frequent impulse buy.

Speaking of e-liquid, here are some tips on how to operate and sell e-liquid from your tasting bar.

A large bulk of your time spent interacting with a customer will be during this process. Customers will decide on hardware rather quickly, but for sampling e-liquid they will always take longer.

From one end, I admit It can get a bit tedious. Especially when you have those people that want to sample each and every flavor you have. but at the same time, liquid tasting is a great opportunity to deepen rapport and really build a connection with your customer.

One of the biggest mistakes I see stores make is they don't capitalize on the opportunity to engage the customer while they're sampling flavors. I've observed this happen on so many occasions. The store employee will just sit there silent, waiting for the customer to ask for flavors, and hardly engages them.

Make an effort to open up a dialogue with your customer, it doesn't even have to be about vaping either. The objective is to make them feel appreciated while building up more rapport.

This is a great opportunity to get to know your customer, and gather more information about them. For example, ask if their friends vape? Right there you have a great Segway into asking for referrals.

Also make an effort to ask them what kind of flavors they like, what nicotine strength. By understanding their preferred flavor and pallet you can provide a more curated experience. This kills two birds with one stone, in that it saves you time providing them with options, while again enhancing their experience.

It also provides an opportunity to get feedback on flavors, and opinions which will help you better understand customer preferences. In turn helping you make better choices on what lines to offer.

Sampling Liquid:

Make sure you sample e-liquid out of a quality sub ohm tank. It may cost a little more due to the quantity of tanks you'll need but its worth it. By utilizing a better quality tank it'll allow customers to experience the flavor better, thus improving sales.

Also keep 2 to 3 atomizers and mods ready for in store use. This is a nice touch for drippers who may want to sample on an atty but not ruin their build.

Also something I've done for the past year which customers love is providing bottles to drip. Keep sample bottles of all your flavors available for drippers to self serve. It's a great touch that caters to the more advanced hobbyist vapers who are going to also be your most frequent customers.

Nicotine levels:

We tend to sample at 0 or 3. I prefer sampling 0 because it provides the full taste without the nicotine kick.

The reason is that the purpose of sampling is to get a feel for the flavor not the nicotine hit. Sampling at a lower strength allows customers to get a much better idea of how the flavor tastes. In turn, for beginners keep a bottle of each nicotine strength available. Use it to help pair a beginner with a nicotine strength that suits them.

And again always be sure to ask if they'd like an additional flavor. Purchasing more liquid is always an easy upsell.

Get personal:

The most effective salesperson I ever had on my team, on average sold nearly double if not more than anybody else. He had no secret, he didn't use some advanced mind control technique, in fact his "secret" was so simple and common sense its almost funny.

Whenever he would get a new customer, he would simply write down their name, what they purchased, and ask for a phone number or e-mail address. He also provided them with his personal contact info and told them they could call him anytime if they had a problem.

Then a few days later he would make a phone call, or e-mail. He wouldn't try selling them on a new promotion or anything. He would just simply ask how they were enjoying their new mod, or e-liquid etc. and then thanked them for coming in.

That's it, its no secret, he just added a personal touch, and he always followed up.

The result was: we had customers who would' literally refuse to be helped by anyone else but him. On top of that his customers always spent more, and made big purchases frequently.

Why does this have such a powerful effect?

Because it accomplishes two things that customers find irresistible:

It established trust, and they felt special.

Its that trust that caused his customers to buy whatever he endorsed, and only purchase from him.

You can use pen and paper, or integrate customer relationship software, whatever you prefer doesn't matter. But if you want to cultivate a strong loyal customer base, apply the simple technique of taking down names, contact information and follow up with new customers.

Its important you follow up, not contact them to sell. There is a difference between the two. Most stores get emails through loyalty programs etc., but they're only used to notify about upcoming promotions and specials. Contacting customers personally has a much more powerful effect.

Referrals:

Leveraging this technique, allows you to also ask for referrals. If you have studied sales or read any books regarding the subject, you know referrals have long been regarded as your most powerful technique in increasing sales.

The secret to referrals? ASKING for them, Its really that simple. People tend to be hesitant to ask because they're afraid it'll come off as pushy to too "salesy". The truth is customers don't mind, especially if they're happy and satisfied. Don't be afraid to ask for referrals, if you're confident that you're providing value, then you don't need to be worried.

Customers will naturally want to spread the word about the awesome new vape shop they found.

People buy the benefits not the features:

Customers purchase products based on the benefits that product provide, not the features itself. This is one of the fundamental rules of sales theory, benefits over features.

People care less about what it does, and more about what it does for them.

Understanding this principle allows you to not only present your products better, but also better satisfy customer expectations. This is an especially important lesson for vaporpreneurs. Because in our product offering there are always so many different choices and options to choose from.

Not only does it confuse customers, but they're also afraid of buying the wrong item. I recall spending hours reading reviews on products trying to decide the "right" one when I was first starting out vaping.

A vaper wants to feel confident and secure that they're buying the right item, applying this principle will allow you to help them achieve that.

<u>So how do you determine a benefit over a feature?</u>

Things like color, materials, size, and price are features. The technical components tend to be features. The benefits are what those features can provide. The way to apply this principle is by leveraging features to demonstrate an advantage which equals a benefit.

For example:

Lets say a customer asks about a particular atomizer, it has adjustable air flow, a very deep deck, and copper contacts.

Everything I listed is a feature. How would you take that information and convey it in a way that that demonstrates a benefit?

Adjustable airflow = Control over flavor/cloud production

Deeper deck = Wick can hold more liquid = less dripping needing

Copper contact = Better conductor of electricity, better performance

By leveraging the features as advantages it provides the customer a clear understanding of what the benefit is.

This is why taking time to build rapport and understand your customer's needs is so important, it allows you to have a better view on what a customer will purchase.

This is especially effective when overcoming price objections, a customer will pay more for a higher priced item if they feel the benefits will solve their problem.

Commission:

I don't advise paying sales staff with commission, it makes things too competitive, causing arguments and taking away from team cohesiveness. Employees will care more about making a sale, rather than focus on providing the right product to a customer.

Instead set challenges and quotas and then offer special bonuses for meeting those.

For example, at my shop if we have $1,000 + sales day bonus everyone that works gets an extra $20 and $50 for $2,000 + sales days. This keeps morale up and motivates them to do their best.

Also we offer bonuses for selling a full set up, and three bottles or more of e-liquid. The bonus structure takes the competitiveness out but keeps people motivated.

Sales in conclusion:

You role as a shop owner is to serve as the go to source of every thing vape related to your local area. You are the expert; the place people turn to when they need help or questions asked.

Therefore, its imperative you and your team consistently educate yourselves and stay up to date on everything in the industry.

Not just technical knowledge but also news regarding trending e-liquids, new products along with industry news regarding regulations and advocacy. Vapers are deeply passionate about their hobby, and one of the reasons they enjoy going to physical stores is the opportunity to talk shop. Build on this and leverage it to grow your customers.

As we discussed, successful and effective selling is about guidance and providing solutions to needs. Your goal isn't to make a sale, but to solve a problem. Keep this as your core sales philosophy and you will not only thrive profit wise but in terms of customer satisfaction.

Practice different sales approaches with your staff, you have to keep the tools sharp as they say. The best sales people our committed to constantly improving their skills.

You're focus is also going to be managing and motivating your team members in sales as well. You as a shop owner, should not be the highest performing sales person. That means you're attention is focused on selling, not managing your business. Don't get me wrong, you should be able to step in when needed and you should also try and get face to face time with customers as well.

But it shouldn't be your main focus. Balance it between your partners and staff. I love to spend time on the sales floor and help customers.

To this day, one of my personal favorite things to do is helping beginners get their first starter set. Yeah I like sitting and talking shop with our regulars, but there's a certain satisfaction helping someone switch from smoking.

It goes back to my first experiences at a vapor shop, that's why I love to help beginners because I want to make sure they get off to a strong start with vaping, and its just fun to see their excitement. But I also know, I have to work "on" my business, not "in" my business.

Chapter 10:
Marketing

Marketing your vape shop:

You can have the most amazing Shop in the world. High end trendy furniture, custom made lighting, giant flat screen TV's, a e-liquid bar that would make Vegas night clubs jealous, shelves full of the most popular e-liquids, every hard to find mod and atomizer, and the lowest prices.

BUT...

Non of that will matter if people don't know about you!

Non of that will matter if you don't get customers!

Non of that will matter if you don't MARKET your business!

So what exactly is "Marketing"

If you were to ask 5 different people what marketing is, you'd get 5 different definitions. They might sound alike, but they'd all be different, and ironically that in itself is actually a good way to explain marketing.

It's a number of activities that are similar in concept, but different in definition.

There's 20,000 different ways to describe and define it, but here's my definition, based on many years of observation as an entrepreneur and a marketing professional:

Marketing is the combined total behaviors, actions and practices a business uses to acquire, maintain and increase customers.

Your Marketing goal as a shop owner:

Now that's the big definition, that's broad and applicable to business overall. But what about your goal; your marketing objective as a shop owner can be broken into two phases.

1. Establish awareness
2. Create engagement

Or another way to put it, get people in the door (establish awareness) and then get them to come back in (Create engagement).

You are a brick and mortar retail store, a fixed physical location in a town or city. You're marketing goal is to get everyone who vapes within a specific radius of miles to come into your store.

All your efforts, promotions etc. should be focused on this single goal.

While you have a single goal, the method to achieve that goal will require more than a single method.

You can't build a house with just a hammer:

Building a house requires multiple tools, and materials. This is the metaphor I like to use when describing the mindset, you need to have as a vaporpreneur. Too often I see small businesses, try building their house with just one tool.

To be an effective marketer there's going to be a number of tools you're going to have to get good at using and also learning how to use them together.

Let's overview the main categories:

Promotions:

Your monthly or weekly specials, your on going sales. Special deals and exclusives. Promotions are incentives designed to influence people to buy a particular item or come in to your store and spend money. Everyone loves a good deal, but don't rely to heavily on constantly offering sales and discounts. Effective marketing is getting customers to pay the full price, not bargains.

Examples: buy one get one half off deals.

Social Media/online marketing:

Any and all businesses, in any industry must rely on social media and the web for marketing, its not an option its a must. This rings more true for the vapor industry since social media is the primary way we interact and engage with the larger vaper community.

Furthermore, you can't pay for advertising on social media. So you have to really focus on creating quality content to build an organic audience.

Building your web and social media presence is a necessity, and something you must devote time towards daily. Set up a profile on the popular social media sites and begin engaging with your customers. Get them to follow you, and use it as a way to interact with them.

Examples: Instagram, Facebook

Direct Marketing/Grass roots:

Utilizing physical materials like flyers or brochures and distributing them around your city. Although this is a bit "old school" in todays digital media age. It can still be an effective method to create awareness and gain exposure to your local community.

Older methods like direct response mail is a bit ineffective for our business. But promoting your shop with a street team at local events like concerts can definitely bring new customers through your door.

Examples: Flyers, posters, street teams

Advertising:

Marketing is often mistaken for advertising and vice versa, But in truth they're two separate things. Advertising is literally its own science as well as its own art form.

It can be considered to be a component under marketing, they are two separate entities, but related.

Marketing is more the quantitative, while advertising is a much more creative process. Ad placement requires money, but is still an effective medium to market your business. The use of print ads in particular has greatly declined with the rise of Social Media. Companies spend billions and billions a year on advertising to customers.

But for small business owners with limited budgets it's a difficult tool to fully utilize especially online. Unfortunately as mentioned earlier, due to miseducation and regulations. It is against ad policy for vape related businesses to advertise on on Facebook or Google.

When you open your store, you'll be bombarded with companies trying to sell ads to you. But in my opinion its not worth wasting money except for a few places such as Yelp which can be a great discovery tool.

Expert marketing:

This means leveraging your knowledge base and expertise to gain exposure. An overall theme of this book has been me reminding you regularly that you have to establish yourself as the go to expert for vaping in your area. Expert marketing is using that to drive in more customers, by offering classes, and lessons. Expert marketing is harnessing your knowledge base and converting it into profit.

P.R./ Events:

Public Relations and events will be one of your most effective tools. Becoming the go to source for local news outlets on vaping and electronic cigarettes. There us a lot of misinformation on vaping in the news today. Especially with the current status of the fda's regulations.

You can get a lot of free press by helping spread awareness about vaping. While also helping the cause by serving as an advocate.

Organizing on going events that cater to your local vaper community is a smart move. Such as cloud contests, vape meets, e-liquid release parties. Though I would caution, given the negative press lately I'd keep cloud contests minimal. Instead opt for a regular vape meet for your most enthusiastic customer base.

When you set up these events, you should be sure to offer some prizes and giveaways, and most importantly raffles.

A raffle is not only appealing to customers, but you can make money from it by selling tickets. Select a high end product, and a few smaller ones, this increases the numbers of winners while giving more incentive to buy raffle tickets.

Leverage events to help establish your store as the go to location for all things vape related.

If you have developed a good relationship with other stores in your area, you can combine for larger events. As I've said before there's no need to be competition, if anything shop owners should establish camaraderie.

Doing co events it shows a strong sense of unity for your local community and benefits everyone.

Once you develop a working relationship with e-liquid brands and other companies, you can ask them to sponsor your events. E-liquid companies are always looking for extra exposure, and will sponsor your event by providing some items for giveaways, prizes etc.

I also think a big opportunity for us as vape industry professionals is to put more time into community outreach and volunteering. Hosting food drives during the holidays, taking time out to volunteer and contribute with local organizations

Events provide an opportunity for you to drive traffic into your doors without the reason being "buy something". Its inviting customers to come join you for a fun event that's engaging, and provides you with the opportunity to brand yourself and enhance customer perception.

Building awareness:

Word of mouth will be your best bet to start, as you build awareness in your community. Traditional grass roots approaches like flyers, and posters etc. will also be effective.

The most powerful tool to building awareness will be social media giving you a broadcast channel that also makes it easy for others to spread the word about you as well.

Building awareness takes hustle, and consistent effort, the law of averages is really at play here. Because the more people to approach and communicate with the more exposure you'll get.

Keep in mind something very important, vapers are all about buzz and hype. If one customer likes your shop and the experience you provide, they will bring 2 of their friends in next time. I've seen it happen again and again. Once you create that buzz your momentum will begin to increase.

The goal of building awareness is not to get sales, its to get people to know you exist. Don't try and accomplish ANYTHING more than that. Don't be a door to door sales person, your aim is to simply notify and announce to people that you exist with the intent of them coming by your shop at some point.

Pro Tip:

Don't wait to begin marketing once the store is set up, you want to begin spreading the buzz as soon as you have things finalized with permits and lease. You don't need to over do it, just start spreading the word through your friends and acquaintances who vape.

Creating engagement:

The term creating "engagement" incorporates so many different things, yet has one end goal. Genuine interaction with customers about topics they find interesting. Emphasis on "genuine", not interaction with an ulterior motive ie: to sell them.

Engagement means providing value, that can be knowledge value, entertainment value etc.

Engaging is not posting on Facebook "hey we have a sale come in and buy stuff" engagement is posting on Facebook a useful video, or helpful tip about vaping and then having a discussion with your followers about it.

Creating engagement requires two areas to focus on:

1. Position:
2. Communication

Positioning your brand means you aim to consistently place your business in their line of site, especially on social media. This means being consistent in posting things on your various social media pages. It means sponsoring a local concert or festival that your customers are going to, it means being visible and accessible.

Communication is how you then interact when your customers engage with you. Are you interactive or do you just bombard social media with photos and status updates?

Do you have discussions with your customers in store? Do you shout them out in photos or tag them? Communication is the quality of the conversation you have with your audience. Customers hate to be sold but they love to buy, Genuine communication strengthens the frequency that your customers will engage with you. Be authentic, put people first, not sales.

Take over the room:

You notice how most people in a crowded room of strangers will only talk to people that they know? They won't engage with people they're not familiar with. But sometimes there's that person who's a social butterfly, that's inviting and not shy, they effortlessly walk into a room and take it over.

People naturally gravitate towards them, they're perceived as cool and popular. You want to be that person, you want to take initiative and begin engaging with your customers.

Turn your customers into brand advocates:

Your marketing goal is to convert your customers into brand advocates, ambassadors that will represent your brand everywhere they go.

Vaping definitely grabs attention, and vapers love to show off their set ups, to other vapers. Its always a conversation starter, either with a fellow vaper or someone curious to try.

When you engage properly and provide value to your customer, they will without a doubt market and advertise for you. Vapers love to give referrals if they're happy with their store. "Go check out my vape shop, they're great, they always hook me up".

For example, one of our most frequent customers at my shop is a group of college students that attend the nearby local university.

This is a group of roughly 12 customers that all vape together, often coming in to shop together, its like a group activity for them. They discovered us all through one of their friends. Who had been one of our first customers who I had personally spent a lot of time talking to. I was asking for feedback on what the local vape scene was like in the new area we had opened in. Just off that one person, 12 regular, loyal customers who also make referrals themselves.

Best of all they LOVE to represent us, they wear our apparel etc.

Effective marketing is making customers so satisfied and happy that they get out there and work for you.

Some thoughts on Social Media:

Social Media will without a doubt be the most consistently used tool in your arsenal for marketing. Its free, and the most effective way to create the greatest reach.

In this day and age its impossible to build a successful business without using it. For vaping, Instagram, and Facebook are the most useful.

Yes, there are other great platforms out there like Twitter, but Instagram and Facebook will be what makes the biggest impacts.

We have discussed engagement and creating awareness, but I'd like to also cover just "how" to get followers and what to do when you get them.

Social Media is not a giant online billboard, it's a communication channel. In other words, its not a monologue, it's a dialogue between you and your audience.

The secret to getting followers:

Consistency, that's what makes all the difference in building a following on social media. There is no shortcut, well at least no shortcut that actually helps in any productive way.

Yes, you can buy followers, but they're fake, it just gives you numbers, that's not creating actual engagement.

Consistency is the key to building followers, daily, frequent effort.

This requires patience and discipline. It will take some time, I know it can be frustrating, but it will payoff in the long run.

You need to be disciplined in devoting time every day to make regular postings, and responding/engaging with your followers. What I've seen happen time and time again is people give up out of frustration and don't develop a consistent posting schedule.

Also when first trying to get followers, don't bombard all your friends. Sure by all means as them to like and share, but do it little by little, and ask personally.

Do not constantly flood your social media profiles with posting about sales, specials etc. It looks desperate and tacky when all you use it for is to advertise, not to mention its rarely effective. Instead focus on posting valuable content, with sales pitches sprinkled in sporadically.

The 5 questions:

There are 5 key questions you have to answer when determining your marketing strategy. Answering these questions will give you the insight needed to determine the direction and areas of focus to concentrate on when marketing your shop.

1. What are my customers needs, what do they want?
2. How can I demonstrate I have what they want
3. What gets my customers attention
4. What are my customer's pains?
5. Why should a customer come into my store?

The answers to these questions should form the core philosophy of your marketing strategy. Your aim is to leverage these answers into presenting a convincing argument to people to come into your shop and be a customer.

Take it one customer at a time:

Opening a business, in any industry is risky. Even in a booming industry like Vaping. Success is far from a sure thing. You want to aim for having an endless customer base, you want to have your store constantly filled with people, and sales through the roof.

But the key to getting there is taking it one customer at a time. The path to thousands of customers is one customer. Take it one person at a time, don't stress out, don't think to far ahead. Do your best, go the extra mile and each person will ad up.

ABM: Always be Marketing

There's an old sales saying "Always be closing" which basically means to always be focused on closing deals. I have my own twist on that applied to what your mentality should be as a vaporpreneur. Always be marketing, always capitalize on an opportunity to create awareness for your shop in your community. Your focus should always be "getting people into your door" traffic flow is critical for your success. The one thing you must place daily effort on is your marketing.

Marketing is building a house, that house is your shop. It's the activity that will have the biggest impact on your success, and on your profits.

Keep that in mind everyday when you enter your shop, and you will have the success you want.

Chapter 11:
Wishing You the Best

Advocacy - last but definitely not the least:

I wanted to save talking about advocacy for the end of this book. I am proud to be an advocate for the industry, through my work with VapeAboutIt.Com.

A lot of the things I've talked about in this book are flexible. Supporting advocacy is not, I'm going to hold you to it.

If you plan to get into this business, you have to make effort to support our advocacy groups.

Why?

Because they are on the front lines each and every day fighting against unfair regulations on this industry. They are working tirelessly to spread awareness and deal with the political system to ensure peoples right to vape.

As a business owner it will be your obligation to support this cause as well. Because if we don't collectively work together, there won't be any more vape industry.

So how can you contribute to the cause?

Simple: spread awareness.

You are on the front lines, shop owners have the most face to face time with consumers. Take advantage of that opportunity to do your part in keeping them informed on what's happening. More importantly help mobilize them to take action.

Also be sure to join the main advocacy groups.

SFATA: The Smoke Free Alternatives Trade Association

http://sfata.org/

CASAA: The Consumer Advocates for Smoke Free Alternatives Association

http://casaa.org/

AVA: American Vaping Association

http://vaping.info/

Stay up to date with them, and be sure to do your part when they release a call for action.

<u>Wishing you the best</u>

I truly hope that you have found this book helpful and that it will serve you as a useful guide in opening your first vape shop.

I've done my best to unload the principles, and knowledge I feel is important to succeeding as a shop owner. By applying the tips and information of this book I'm confident that you will get the results you want.

We are truly in an amazing industry, there is just so much opportunity that lies ahead as vaping continues to grow and expand. What you make of that opportunity is entirely up to you. You will get what you put in, maximum results will require maximum effort, but it will all be so worth it.

Congratulate yourself for finishing this book, because you just took a first step forward. Plus you'd be surprised how often people statistically don't actually finish reading a book. But more importantly you deserve to be congratulated for making the decision to take part in this amazing revolution.

You decided you don't just want to sit on the sidelines and observe. But you actually want to take on the challenge and responsibility to make an impact in it.

You have decided to take on a huge risk, and by doing so you're contributing to the growth and success of our industry as a whole, and for that you have my deepest respect.

Because each shop that opens is another positive step forward, each store that succeeds and thrives is another step towards achieving the larger mission of spreading awareness and education of vaping.

Each shop that opens, is the potential for lives saved, and each customer you help make the switch from smoking is one less pack of cigarettes sold a day.

Your success as a vaporpreneur will not only enhance your quality of life. But also enhance the quality of life for your customers in your community. And now get ready, because there's work to be done, and your journey is just getting started!

The time is now to make your dreams happen, and your shop is the vehicle towards realizing those ambitions. Take this book, learn it, apply it and most importantly of all HUSTLE, hustle your ass off.

There will be times that things get frustrating, when you feel fatigued. I know it can get overwhelming, trust me I've been there. But that's when you have to remind yourself why you signed up for this, remind yourself that this is more than just a business, Remind yourself that this is your passion, and remember most importantly of all that your saving lives.

I hope you've gotten what you wanted out of this book and I look forward to one day visiting your shop. Please feel free to send me feedback or suggestions, as I'm sure I'll be revising this book as the industry continues to grow. I look forward to the opportunity of networking and working together to build our industry.

I can be reached at directly at:

Sham@VapeAboutIt.com

Stay focused, work hard, and then work a littler harder. Thank you again for the opportunity to serve as your guide, wishing you all the very best.

Best regards,
Sham Shivaie

Made in the USA
Coppell, TX
24 November 2020

41993890R00094